WHAT PEOPLE A

THE LONG RO

A pilgrimage in good company whils.   ....g the Scriptures prayerfully will be familiar to many groups of Christians in Lent. In this course about salvation, we are also invited to watch a film as attentively as we might look at a painting. Characters who are not knowingly on a journey to find God are found by God in a life-changing encounter. They are what salvation looks like in this imaginative, creative and enjoyable Lent course that will lead us to new life at Easter.

The Rt Revd Nicholas Holtam, Bishop of Salisbury

Kierkegaard quipped that God did not become man to make small talk. He would have enjoyed Tim Heaton's *The Long Road to Heaven*, which skilfully and accessibly introduces big talk on several levels. It proves a bracing mix of Bible study and wide-ranging theological insight, all rooted in reflection on the film *The Way* and nicely seasoned with Bonhoeffer's *Prayers for Fellow-Prisoners*. Substantial reflection on the Way of St James to Santiago de Compostela prompts a moving pilgrimage from one's personal Good Friday through to Easter Day, the quintessence of a salvation which proves challenging, affirming and surprising.

The Rt Revd David Wilbourne, Assistant Bishop of Llandaff

On the pilgrimage road to Santiago de Compostela we meet Tom and a small group of misfits, each broken and looking for meaning in their lives. At the same time, travelling with Jesus on the road to Jerusalem we meet on the way people transformed by the encounter. A wonderful treasure trove of nuggets drawn from a rich heritage of Christian wisdom through the centuries nourishes us as we explore the many facets of salvation. Over five sessions we are challenged to see salvation lived out in the stories of others and to reflect how God's salvation is woven into our own lives.

The Rt Revd John Wraw, Bishop of Bradwell

Tim Heaton's intriguing new Lent Course takes the theme of pilgrimage, winding word and prayer around the pictures of the film *The Way*. In the film, four pilgrims join their different lives as they walk to Santiago de Compostela. St Paul wrote, in *Philippians*, that he was pressing on in order to know Christ and the power of his resurrection: pressing on because he had not "already reached the goal". In our Lenten pilgrimage we seek to know more of Christ Jesus, as he already knows us. This course will help us all. And when you have finished the course perhaps you may be inspired to put on your walking boots, lock the front door, and set off for Santiago yourself.

The Rt Revd Dr Edward Condry, Bishop of Ramsbury

Salvation is all about journeying or, as it is often named, pilgrimage. Using the brilliant film *The Way*, Tim Heaton helps us understand that finding heaven is as much about the journey as it is about the arriving. Through careful interweaving of Jesus' journey to the cross with the journeys of the characters in the film, the course reminds us that we are all somewhere on a journey and on that journey we have the possibility, through the grace of God, of finding salvation. This is an outstanding and exciting course that I strongly recommend. It is extremely well constructed, imaginatively presented and well written, and goes right to the heart of what it means to be a Christian disciple.

The Venerable Paul Taylor, Archdeacon of Sherborne

Pilgrimage defines both the form and content of this Lent Course: it is designed to move us on in every way, in mind, spirit and body. It does so very effectively, by imaginatively weaving together a film about a journey and Christian understandings of the journey of salvation. The course draws on wide-ranging and serious theological resources, but also retains a sufficiently light touch to keep the pilgrim moving whenever the going might seem tough. The material is thoughtful and engaging, the format attractive, and the overall experience for participants should be very stimulating.

The Revd Canon Professor Vernon White, Canon Theologian of Westminster Abbey and Visiting Professor in Theology at King's College, London

The Long Road to Heaven

A Lent Course Based on the Film
The Way

The Long Road to Heaven

A Lent Course Based on the Film
The Way

Tim Heaton

Winchester, UK
Washington, USA

First published by Circle Books, 2013
Circle Books is an imprint of John Hunt Publishing Ltd., Laurel House, Station Approach,
Alresford, Hants, SO24 9JH, UK
office1@jhpbooks.net
www.johnhuntpublishing.com
www.circle-books.com

For distributor details and how to order please visit the 'Ordering' section on our website.

Text copyright: Tim Heaton 2013

ISBN: 978 1 78279 274 1

A CIP catalogue record for this book is available from the British Library.

Design: Stuart Davies

Cover image of Martin Sheen copyright David Alexanian/The Way Productions LLC.
Reproduced with permission.

Printed and bound by CPI Group (UK) Ltd, Croydon, CR0 4YY

We operate a distinctive and ethical publishing philosophy in all
areas of our business, from our global network of authors to
production and worldwide distribution.

CONTENTS

BY THE SAME AUTHOR

The Naturalist and the Christ: A Lent Course Based on the Film
Creation
(Circle Books, 2011)

A remarkable piece of work
Church Times

A fantastic Lent resource
The Good BookStall

A stimulating and enjoyable read
Newslink, the Diocese of Durham

Utterly contemporary ... engaging and accessible
The Coracle, the Diocese of Truro

An extremely fruitful way into areas which most Christians barely grasp
The Sarum Link, the Diocese of Salisbury

A reassuringly familiar Lenten journey
Crux, the Diocese of Manchester

This is a course for twenty-first century Christians and I commend it warmly
The Rt Revd Stephen Conway, Bishop of Ely

Carefully researched, elegantly written and well-presented
The Rt Revd Dr Graham Kings, Bishop of Sherborne

Exciting and challenging
The Rt Revd Tim Thornton, Bishop of Truro

Thorough and thought-provoking
The Venerable Stephen Waine, Archdeacon of Dorset

An impressive piece of work ... entirely readable
The Revd Canon Edward Probert, Chancellor of Salisbury Cathedral

*A valuable resource to us in the world as it is – full of pain and suffering –
not the world as we would like it to be*
The Revd Sally Bedborough, Hospice Chaplain

A comprehensive and thoroughly excellent resource
Karenza Passmore, Director of the North East Religious Learning
Resources Centre

For Arabella

My companion on the road

Chapter One

Introduction

Is not this the fast that I choose:
to loose the bonds of injustice,
to undo the thongs of the yoke,
to let the oppressed go free,
and to break every yoke?

(Isaiah 58.6, *Ash Wednesday, Years A, B and C*)

We know from the Acts of the Apostles that "the Way" was the name by which the Christian Church was first known. Followers of Christ "belonged to the Way" (Acts 9.2) and it was not until the founding of the church at Antioch in Syria that they came to be known as "Christians" (Acts 11.26). The Way was the way to salvation, the road that leads to life (Matthew 7.14).

Concern for salvation is at the heart of the Christian faith and is addressed throughout most of the New Testament writings. Christianity is a religion of salvation, although it is not alone in this; many (but not all) world religions have concepts of salvation. Salvation is not, therefore, a specifically Christian idea and Christianity is not in any sense distinctive or unique in attaching importance to the notion of salvation.

The Biblical concept of salvation is deeply rooted in the exodus from Egypt: God's liberation of the Hebrew slaves was the first defining episode in salvation history. In the exodus (from the Greek *ex* meaning "out" and *hodos* "road", literally "the road out"), God acted decisively to free his chosen people, the descendants of Abraham, Isaac and Jacob, leading them out of captivity and forming them into a holy nation from whom one day would be raised a saviour for the whole world. Freed from

Egyptian slavery, they began the long march from the land of bondage through the desert towards Mount Sinai, where Israel would receive the gift of the Ten Commandments and acknowledge no master but God. Eventually, after forty years wandering in the wilderness, they would finally enter the Promised Land of Canaan under the leadership of Joshua, the successor of Moses.

Seven hundred years after the exodus, the inhabitants of Judah found themselves once more under bondage in a foreign land, this time Babylon. The Babylonian exile, which lasted until the third generation of deportees, was followed by a homecoming – a new exodus – that elicits many parallels with the exodus from Egypt. This was the second defining episode in God's salvation history and an act of deliverance surpassing even the first in its glory:

> Do not remember the former things, or consider the things of old. I am about to do a new thing; now it springs forth, do you not perceive it? I will make a way in the wilderness and rivers in the desert ... to give drink to my chosen people, the people whom I formed for myself so that they might declare my praise. (Isaiah 43.18-21, abridged)

It is perhaps no surprise then to find, throughout the New Testament, images of salvation in Christ drawing on the motif of freedom from slavery and oppression. Jesus says, "Very truly, I tell you, everyone who commits sin is a slave to sin" (John 8.34). And Peter writes in his Second Letter, "[False teachers] promise [people] freedom, but they themselves are slaves of corruption; for people are slaves to whatever masters them" (2 Peter 2.19). Slavery to sin and corruption, the default position in which human beings find themselves, has terrible consequences. Sin is a cruel master and offers only death to its slaves, as Paul makes clear:

Do you not know that if you present yourselves to anyone as obedient slaves, you are slaves of the one whom you obey, either of sin, which leads to death, or of obedience, which leads to righteousness? But thanks be to God that you ... having been set free from sin, have become slaves of righteousness. (Romans 6.16-18, abridged)

Through Christ an alternative is available to slavery to sin and "slavery by the fear of death" (Hebrews 2.15): slavery to righteousness, which offers a life free from the power of sin and death. It is an absolute choice between two opposing masters, because "no one can serve two masters" (Matthew 6.24).

This idea of liberation from slavery to sin and death is extended also to release from slavery to the Law. Again Paul says, "For freedom Christ has set us free. Stand firm, therefore, and do not submit again to a yoke of slavery" (Galatians 5.1). The "yoke" was a rabbinic metaphor for the difficult but joyous task of obedience to Mosaic Law, a burden to be shouldered gladly by God's people in order to attain righteousness and salvation. One of the many requirements of the Law was circumcision: "Unless you are circumcised according to the custom of Moses, you cannot be saved," said some Jewish converts who had come from Judea to Antioch whilst Paul and Barnabas were there (Acts 15.1). This became a bitter dispute, to be settled later in the Council of Jerusalem, at which Peter stood up and said:

Why are you [believers who belonged to the sect of the Pharisees] putting God to the test by placing on the neck of the disciples a yoke that neither our ancestors nor we have been able to bear? On the contrary, we believe that we will be saved through the grace of the Lord Jesus, just as they will. (Acts 15.10-11)

Making a clear contradistinction to the yoke of slavery to the

Law, James "the Just", the brother of Jesus and leader of the church in Jerusalem, used the phrase "the law of liberty" to describe the salvation available through Christ (James 2.12). Jesus himself also made use of the rabbinic metaphor for the Jewish Law: "They [the scribes and the Pharisees] tie up heavy burdens, hard to bear, and lay them on the shoulders of others" (Matthew 23.4). And, most famously of all:

> Come to me, all you that are weary and are carrying heavy burdens, and I will give you rest. Take my yoke upon you, and learn from me; for I am gentle and humble in heart, and you will find rest for your souls. For my yoke is easy, and my burden is light. (Matthew 11.28-30)

So against the backcloth of history, of exodus and exile, Jesus, Peter, Paul and James all took up the motif of freedom from slavery – slavery to sin and death and the yoke of slavery to the Law – as images of God's salvation in Christ. The evangelists also drew repeatedly on details in the exodus story and turned them around to point towards Jesus.

In the Institution of the Eucharist at the Last Supper, which (according to the synoptic gospels) was the annual Jewish Passover meal commemorating the escape from Egypt, Jesus uses the great symbols of that ritual meal – the "bread of affliction" (unleavened bread) and the "cup of salvation" – as metaphors for his body and blood. According to First Corinthians, the earliest Biblical account of the Institution of the Lord's Supper, Jesus commanded his disciples to eat that bread and drink that cup in remembrance of him (1 Corinthians 11.23-26). *I am the bread of affliction, the bread of freedom and redemption. I am the cup of salvation; it is my blood, my sacrifice, my death that will release you from your bonds and set you free.*

The Fourth Gospel does not give us the Institution of the Eucharist in the same way because, according to John's chronology, the Last Supper was not the festive Passover meal but an ordinary supper on the previous day, "the day of Preparation for the Passover" (John 19.14). Accordingly, the symbolic bread and cup of the Passover meal were not present. John, however, does not miss the connection between the salvation of the exodus and the sacrifice of Jesus' body on the cross. The day after the feeding of the five thousand, Jesus contrasts his role as the true giver of life with the manna – the "bread from heaven" (Exodus 16.4) – that rained down on the Israelites in the wilderness to give them temporary sustenance. Jesus tells the crowd who came looking for him:

> I am the bread of life. Your ancestors ate the manna in the wilderness, and they died. This is the bread that comes down from heaven, so that one may eat of it and not die. I am the living bread that came down from heaven. Whoever eats of this bread will live forever; and the bread that I will give for the life of the world is my flesh. (John 6.48-51)

Except for two people, Joshua and Caleb, the generation that left Egypt never entered the Promised Land of Canaan, not even Moses their leader. They spent the next forty years wandering in the desert and died there. One of the things about manna was that it didn't keep. The Israelites had to gather it up within hours otherwise it went off; they were given it for the time of need not for eternity. Now Jesus declares that people's needs and longings are met in him: "I am the bread of life." Metaphors that pointed to God in the Old Testament now point to God through Jesus. Jesus reveals himself as the bread of life, sent from heaven by God, to feed us every step of the way and for eternity. He is the food that sustains us and nourishes us and gives us life. What people need for life is available in Jesus, and this bread never goes off and never runs out.

About the Course

As we have seen, salvation suggests deliverance, liberation, freedom, release, restoration and homecoming, powerful images of salvation firmly rooted in the exodus of the Hebrew slaves from Egypt and Israel's later return from exile in Babylon, the first two defining episodes in God's salvation history. And this is no mere escapism: "Deliverance belongs to the LORD!" (Jonah 2.9).

Yet salvation is not only about what God *has done* in the past; it is about what God *is doing* now and what God *will do* in the future. The story of the exodus has provided inspiration throughout history to people suffering under oppression and slavery, from the enslaved African people in the southern states of the USA before their emancipation in 1865, to the poor and marginalised of South America a century later who gave voice to what is known as "liberation theology". The lyrics of the Negro spirituals – the "spiritual songs" (Ephesians 5.19) of the enslaved Africans in America – return again and again to "my home", "Sweet Canaan", "the Promised Land". This free country was on the northern side of the Ohio River, which they called "the River Jordan". *Michael Row the Boat Ashore* is a well-known example of their dream expressed in spiritual song.

The story of God's people was taken up once more by Martin Luther King, the champion of racial justice during the American civil rights movement of the 1960s. In Memphis, Tennessee, on 3 April 1968, the eve of his assassination, he proclaimed:

I've been to the mountain top ... And I've looked over. And I've seen the promised land. I may not get there with you. But I want you to know tonight, that we, as a people will get to the promised land. And I'm happy, tonight. I'm not worried about anything. I'm not fearing any man. Mine eyes have seen the glory of the coming of the Lord. (www.seto.org)

I'd like to take you on a journey to the Promised Land. It's a journey through Lent that starts in the Judean desert and leads to Golgotha. It's the journey that Jesus made from his baptism in the River Jordan to his betrayal, arrest, trial, and crucifixion in Jerusalem, and it's the story of our salvation.

At the same time we'll take a parallel journey, following the fortunes of a group of pilgrims walking *el Camino de Santiago*, "the Way of St James". The characters are from the film *The Way* and on this pilgrimage, as on any other, the travelling becomes as important as the destination. Beginning with Abraham, the theme of journeying is an ancient one in the Church and provides a reason for the practice of pilgrimage. Like the story of salvation, which has always been told in the context of a deep emptiness and yearning, pilgrimage stems from an aching and longing to be nearer to God. The physical act of movement is seen to aid an inward journey of closer encounter with God; pilgrimage is a journey of inner transformation that brings us nearer to our true home.

Pilgrimage is a metaphor for life: an unsafe path towards the eternal home. "Being 'on the way' includes, and gives a name to, a fundamental situation of human existence" (Müller and Fernández de Aránguiz 2010:xv). Our whole life from cradle to grave – and beyond – is a personal journey that can be likened to a literal pilgrimage to a sacred place, on which we encounter many hardships and joys, highs and lows, along the way. The true path of pilgrimage is the course of one's life, and life as a pathway ends with the culminating experience of being united with God. Life is a journey crowned with a goal, and our true goal is the God from whom we have come and to whom we shall return. Yet many of the benefits of a pilgrimage are to be found not at the destination itself but on the road getting there – not least the kindness of strangers. There are many blessings to be counted, and when our hope of arrival is fulfilled we are just as likely to be giving thanks for what we have already received on the way as for what we receive when we get there.

The gospels tell us about Jesus' journey around Palestine; his disciples learn from him as they travel along and Jesus himself is challenged and changed by his encounters on the way. Eventually he sets his face towards Jerusalem and his destination on the cross (Luke 9.51). The one who has been sent by God, Jesus, the traveller-on-the-road, has called us to journey with him to the sacred place. As we follow some of the gospel readings set for the first five Sundays of Lent, we will meet some of the characters he encounters along the way: John the Baptist, Nicodemus, the Samaritan woman, the man blind from birth, and Lazarus. With their help, and with the help of the characters we meet in the film, we will explore further the whole concept of salvation.

Pilgrimage, like salvation itself, is not a uniquely Christian concept; it is a religious devotion observed in all major world religions. Hindus make pilgrimages to the Ganges, Jews to Jerusalem, Buddhists to the Himalayas, Muslims to Mecca, and Sikhs to Amritsar. For Christians, the Way of St James is a spiritual journey that pilgrims (or *peregrinos*) have made for over a thousand years. Millions have done it and many have lost their lives in the process, travelling from every corner of Christendom to the Shrine of St James the Apostle at Santiago de Compostela in the region of Galicia in northwest Spain. In medieval times, the *Camino Inglés*, the "Way of the English", involved just a short walk from A Coruña after a long journey by sea. From southern Spain pilgrims took the *Via de la Plata*, which started in Seville, whilst further west was the *Camino Portugués*, the "Way of the Portuguese". But these were only minor routes. From all over the rest of Europe pilgrims converged on four principal routes traversing France, beginning in Paris, Vézelay, Le Puy and Arles. These branches of the Way cross the Pyrenees Mountains along the French-Spanish border and unite in a small Navarran town called Puente la Reina, "Bridge of the Queen". From here a single route, the *Camino Francés* or "Way of the French", strikes west through the cathedral cities of Burgos and León to the great Cathedral of St James in Santiago de Compostela, where a Pilgrims Mass is held at noon each day. The most popular route for pilgrims today starts just on the French side of the Pyrenees at St-Jean-Pied-de-Port, "St John at the Foot of the Pass". The distance from here to Santiago is 762 kilometres (474 miles).

Thousands of pilgrims of all ages and backgrounds make this journey every year, either on foot, on horseback or by bicycle, following the yellow arrows and stone markers that indicate the Way and staying overnight in the pilgrim refuges (*refugios* or *albergues*) that cater specifically for these weary travellers. Around 100,000 people each year register as having completed the final 100 kilometres of the route on foot or on horseback (or 200 kilometres by bicycle), either in a religious spirit or with a spiritual concern, to qualify for a certificate called the *Compostela*. On foot, covering an average of fifteen miles each day, one could walk the whole route across northern Spain in a month. Some (like me) "cheat" and do it in a week, largely by car or coach, but it remains a pilgrimage nonetheless.

Pilgrims travel the Camino for various reasons – religious, cultural, historical or sporting. Some are seeking healing or self-discovery, others adventure. In the film *The Way* we meet Tom (played by Martin Sheen), a Californian ophthalmologist, who comes to St-Jean-Pied-de-Port to repatriate the body of his son Daniel (played by Sheen's real-life son Emilio Estevez) who was killed in the Pyrenees in a storm whilst walking the Camino. Rather than return home, Tom decides to have Daniel's body cremated and embarks on the pilgrimage himself, carrying his son's ashes, to honour Daniel's desire to complete the journey. Although Tom sets out with the intention of doing it solely for his son, he eventually becomes aware of what it means for his own restoration. He also discovers that he cannot make this journey without others – however much he tries initially to shut them out. Along the Way he meets a Dutchman, a Canadian woman and an Irishman, all carrying their own burdens and searching for a greater meaning for their lives. Tom's desire to be alone with his grief leads to growing tensions, and it becomes for all of them a journey of personal discovery that transforms their lives. It also proves to be the way in which Tom comes to terms – so far as anyone really can – with the death of his son.

Through the breaking of bread with strangers and a realization of their common humanity, these wounded and broken individuals find healing. They find their deliverance, liberation, freedom and release; they find their salvation. Each week of the course, with their help and the help of the characters Jesus meets on his journey from the Jordan River to Jerusalem, we will try to answer one of these five questions:

Five Questions

What are we saved from?

What are we saved for?

Who can be saved?

What do we have to do to be saved?

How are we saved?

How to Do the Course

The course comprises five group sessions of ninety minutes each. Each session involves watching two clips from the DVD *The Way* (Icon Home Entertainment, 2011), which then become the focus for discussion.

Try to give the same attention to the film as you would if you were studying a painting, treating it as an art form in its own right. Regard each film clip not only as a springboard to wider discussion but also as a unique feast of image and sound, a contribution loaded with its own meaning and emotion. There is theological depth to be found here too, so in the five minutes of "brainstorming" after each film clip try to unpack fully what you have just seen and heard and the effect it may have had on you.

Before each group session there is a small amount of reading for you to do (the "Prelude"), which should help prepare you for some of the topics that come up for discussion in the group session. Here are a few ideas about how to do the course:

The first thing I want you to do is have some fun – don't confuse study with penance! Lent is about "taking things on" (study and almsgiving) as well as "giving things up" (fasting and self-denial). There's no reason at all why this course shouldn't be fun, an opportunity to spend some time in the company of others in a relaxed and friendly environment. So try to enjoy the course, because then I think you will engage better with it and get more out of it in the end.

Try as best as you can to interact with the other people doing this course with you. More than anything else this means actively listening to what other people have to say, rather than always thinking about what you are going to say next. If you keep this in mind you will learn not only from what the course itself has to say but also from what your fellow participants have to say – and they will hopefully learn something from you. It goes without saying that this is the principal benefit of doing a Lent course as part of a church group, rather than simply reading a spiritual book at home as a purely private Lenten devotion.

Give everyone a chance to have their say. Some people need more time to think than others, or are naturally quieter and more reserved and need time to pluck up courage to say something in a group situation. Try to give them that time; don't feel that you have to blurt something out every time there is an awkward silence after a question has been asked, because you might be getting in just before them (again!) and denying them the oppor-tunity to share with the group their views and experiences.

Treat everyone with consideration and interest. Respect other people's viewpoints even if you don't necessarily agree with them.

Remember that very often there is no right or wrong answer to the questions posed by this course; we are dealing here with great mysteries. Say what you want to say and you might just be uttering a most profound theological truth! And don't be scared by the word "theology"; it simply means "talk about God". What we are doing on this course is talking about God; we are "doing" theology. (To be more specific, what we are also doing on this course is "soteriology", the branch of theology concerned with salvation, a word derived from the Greek *soteria* meaning "salvation".)

Don't be afraid to ask questions, no matter how simple or difficult you think they are. There's a good chance that someone else wanted to ask the same question but was too afraid to ask, and they will thank you for asking it.

Read the "Prelude" that begins each week of the course before attending the group session. If you don't, you might find that you are a bit behind the rest of the group and unable to participate fully in the discussion.

Having said that, don't read ahead. Take each week as it comes and try not to read the whole course in Week One however eager you are! If you do, you might find yourself ahead of the rest of the group and looking a bit smarter than everyone else.

Some of the things that are said in the group sessions will be best kept within the group. Some painful, personal experiences may well be aired, so respect confidentiality and remember that the things you hear are for your ears only. Make the group sessions a safe place to be open and honest with each other. Remember that speaking from experience will always be more valuable to the group than speaking in a purely theoretical way.

Finally, try to frame the course within the worship offered by your church during Lent. Try to get to church on Ash Wednesday as a way of marking the start of the course, and on Maundy Thursday and Good Friday in Holy Week after the course has ended. I've always found it rather strange that many people in my church, who show up every Sunday without fail, don't attend on these most holy of Holy Days. Easter Day, when it arrives in all its glory, will be even more special if you do. The final chapter of this book, *El Camino*, is a short story that you might like to read in Easter Week as you walk with the risen Lord.

So perhaps, before we begin, we can draw up 10 "Rules of Engagement". At the start of the first group session you will be asked to confirm that you have read them and that you agree to them:

Rules of Engagement

1. I will have some fun!
2. I will try to learn something from everyone in the group.
3. I will give everyone else a chance to have their say.
4. I will respect other people's viewpoints even if I disagree.
5. I will try to "do" some theology.
6. I won't be afraid to ask questions.
7. I will read the Prelude before each group session.
8. I won't read too far ahead.
9. I will keep confidential the things that I hear in the group.
10. I will try to get to church as often as I can during Lent.

If you are going to be a group leader please read on. If not, skip to the next chapter, *St James "the Great" and Santiago de Compostela*. Read this, then the Prelude to Week One, before the first group session. Bring a Bible with you to the group sessions and remember – enjoy it!

A Guide for Leaders

The course comprises five group sessions of ninety minutes each, which ideally should be held at the same time each week for five weeks. It is advisable to run each session more than once, e.g. morning, afternoon and evening, to give people the chance of attending when it suits them best. If you expect that large numbers will want to do the course, you will need to lay on multiple sessions to keep each group to a manageable size. A good group size in my experience is 10-15 people; anything less than this can be off-putting for those who want to "keep a low profile", and with more than this it is hard for everyone to have the chance to participate fully.

Before the Course

Well in advance and together with others who are going to be group leaders, decide on the dates and times for the course. Ideally, start the course in the week immediately following Ash Wednesday and get a session in each week (Lent 1 – Lent 5) so as to finish before the start of Holy Week. Check for any clashes with other important local events; if the village pantomime is coming up and everyone in the community is either going to be in it or watching it, avoid clashing with rehearsal and performance times – you are likely to be the loser!

Choose the venues, check availability and book them. The church hall is fine so long as it is warm (heating *will* be required!), but if someone is willing to host a group in their home then I think this provides an altogether more friendly and comfortable setting. The room needs to be large enough to accommodate the group around a large TV set (or a screen if you are using a video projector).

Advertise the course as widely as you can – on posters, in your church and community magazines, pew sheets and from the pulpit. Try to whip up some excitement and enthusiasm about the course and make a point of inviting people who have not done a Lent course before; many regular churchgoers think "that's not something I do" and it's necessary to try to break that mindset.

Ask people to sign up to the course – and which particular day/time in the week they want to come – rather than have them simply turn up on the day. You will need to know *in advance* the numbers attending so that you can buy and distribute sufficient copies of this book before the course begins (there is important reading to do before the first group session). Also, if the evening session, say, is getting very full, then you will be able to lay on an additional evening session to keep the groups to a manageable size.

Buy the right number of copies of this book from your usual bookshop or through <www.circle-books.com>. Couples doing the course will probably want to share a copy rather than have one each. Decide whether you are going to ask participants to pay for the book themselves, or whether the church will either pay completely or subsidise the cost. Distribute the books *before* the start of the course so that participants have a chance to read what they have to read before the first group session, but bring some spare books along to the first session just in case.

Buy a copy of the DVD *The Way* from your usual DVD store. It may be useful to have more than one copy if you are holding several sessions each week with different leaders and in multiple locations.

Source the equipment you need. The TV set obviously needs to be the largest you can lay your hands on, probably not less than 32 inches even for a small group but the bigger the better. The DVD player should, if at all possible, have a time counter display (which some smaller machines do not) so that you can find more easily the start and end points of each film clip. These are given in the table "Film Clip Start and End Points". Make sure that you (or the host) familiarise yourself with the working of the equipment and practise finding the start and end points of the film clips before each group session.

It is not essential that participants watch the whole film before starting the course but they might find it helpful to do so. Consider arranging a viewing of the film before the course begins – with popcorn and drinks of course!

Encourage participants to go to church on Ash Wednesday as a way of marking the start of the course, and perhaps distribute the books to them as they leave. Those who have not signed up to do the course may feel they are missing out on something and decide to join a group after all.

During the Course

Don't worry if you have never led a group before. You are not expected to know all the answers and often there *is* no right or wrong answer. Your role is simply to facilitate the group – to get discussion going and keep the session moving along. Let others do the talking and only chip in yourself if the discussion stalls or if you need to bring the conversation back on the right track. Give everyone the chance to respond to what they have seen and heard, and the opportunity to ask questions. If you cannot answer a question thrown your way don't try to "bluff it"; it's better to admit ignorance or, better still, get someone else to answer it! Try not to impose your own ideas too often or answer your own questions, and try to make everyone feel welcome, comfortable and relaxed.

Above all, keep an eye on the clock. The best way to ensure that no one comes back for the second session is to allow the first to run badly overtime, or finish the ninety minutes having only tackled the first question! The timings suggested for each part of the session, and the clock in the left margin, should help you keep things on track. You must of course allow some flexibility, but be firm when necessary in moving on to the next item. It may mean bringing to an end a vibrant conversation when it is clear that people still have things they are bursting to say, but this is an important part of your role as leader.

You may wish to start each group session with this or another suitable prayer:

Blessed are you, Lord God of our salvation,
to you be praise and glory for ever.
As a man of sorrows and acquainted with grief
your only Son was lifted up
that he might draw the whole world to himself.
May we walk this day in the way of the cross
and always be ready to share its weight,
declaring your love for all the world.
Blessed be God, Father, Son and Holy Spirit.
Blessed be God for ever.

(Prayer of Thanksgiving in Passiontide, *Common Worship: Daily Prayer*)

Each session then follows the same symmetrical pattern, which looks like this:

Group Session		
0.00	Bible Study	10 minutes
0.10	Film Clip 1	5 minutes
0.15	Brainstorm	5 minutes
0.20	Group Discussion	10 minutes
0.30	In Small Groups	10 minutes
0.40	Feedback and Share	5 minutes

```
┌─────────────────────────────────────────────────────────┐
│                        HALF TIME                         │
│                                                          │
│   0.45      Film Clip 2                  5 minutes       │
│   0.50      Brainstorm                   5 minutes       │
│   0.55      Group Discussion             10 minutes      │
│   1.05      In Small Groups              10 minutes      │
│   1.15      Feedback and Share           5 minutes       │
│   1.20      Meditation and Prayer        10 minutes      │
│                                                          │
└─────────────────────────────────────────────────────────┘
```

Bible Study

This is time for the group to think and talk about the Bible passage that begins the Prelude to each weekly session. Aim to make some connections between the "word" and the "world", understanding not only the passage and its context but also how it applies to our present situation and experience. (In Week One this time is used instead as a period of welcome and introduction.)

Film Clip

Show the film clip, using the guide below to find the right start and end points. Because the characters in the film are a cosmopolitan bunch – American, Dutch, Canadian, Irish, French and Spanish – some of the dialogue can be quite hard to hear. It would, therefore, be a good idea to have the subtitles switched on. Select this option from the Main Menu (position the dot below ON then press OK/Enter), and remember to do this *every time* before you make the scene selection.

Film Clip Start and End Points

WEEK 1   Film Clip 1

> *Start* Scene 2. FF to 0.15. Start at the scene of Tom

knocking on Captain Henri's door at night.

End On the wooden signpost indicating "Camino de Santiago" (0.20).

Film Clip 2

Start Scene 3. FF to 0.25. Start at the scene of Tom and Joost sitting at a table outside the *refugio* after dark.

End After Tom says, "My son", and Joost stops dead in his tracks (0.31).

WEEK 2 **Film Clip 1**

Start Scene 4. FF to 0.34. Start at the scene of Tom sitting alone at a table outside the *albergue* after dark.

End As Sarah heads off in the morning with her rucksack on her back (0.39).

Film Clip 2

Start At the beginning of Scene 6 (0.52, waking up in the *refugio*).

End On the map showing "Pamplona" (0.58).

WEEK 3 **Film Clip 1**

Start Scene 7. FF to 1.07. Start at the scene of the sun rising over the hill.

End As the four are walking through a vineyard (1.12).

Film Clip 2

Start Scene 8. FF to 1.14. Start at the scene of the waiters bringing the table in out of the rain.

End After Jack says, "You can thank my credit card" (1.20).

WEEK 4 **Film Clip 1**

Start Scene 9. FF to 1.32. Start at the scene of Jack walking through the iron gates followed by Joost, just as the music begins.

End As the four are standing outside the Parador

Hotel and the music begins to fade (1.36).

Film Clip 2

Start Scene 10. FF to 1.41. Start at the scene of the four walking in single file with a stubble field in the foreground.

End On the map showing "Santiago de Compostela" (1.46).

WEEK 5 **Film Clip 1**

Start Scene 10. FF to 1.47. Start at the scene of the four approaching the bronze statues overlooking Santiago de Compostela.

End After the glimpse of Daniel on the ropes of the *botafumeiro* when the scene changes to the outside of the cathedral (1.52).

Film Clip 2

Start At the beginning of Scene 12 (1.55, a large crowd of tourists heading for the cathedral).

End After Tom has scattered the last of Daniel's ashes and is walking back towards the church by the sea (1.59).

Brainstorm

Having watched the film clip, ask the group to say what they found interesting or thought-provoking about it. Ask if there are any issues or questions it raises for them, or if there was anything they didn't understand and would like to have clarified. Encourage the group to think about the film clip as an art form in its own right: what about its use of camera, lighting, colour, script, score, location and character portrayal? What about the way the scenes are juxtaposed or intercut?

Group Discussion

This is for the whole group to discuss as one. Give everyone the freedom to speak; be aware of a few people dominating the conversation and try to give as many people as possible the chance to be heard. Aim to encourage and affirm every participant and bring everyone into the discussion, but don't put undue pressure on those who would rather remain silent. Welcome any contribution from a quieter member. If the discussion stalls go back to something that came up in the brainstorming.

In Small Groups

Divide the group into small groups of three or four; this is preferable to pairs because some people find it quite awkward being one-to-one. People who were a little reticent about speaking up in the group discussion (or who didn't get a chance!) will now have the opportunity to contribute something. Keep the small groups the same in subsequent sessions as they will get to bond with each other and feel they are in a safe place. When people break into small groups for the first time in each session this is your chance to set the DVD to the right place for film clip 2.

Feedback and Share

Call the group back together and invite each small group to feedback and share what they have been discussing. Let them know that they don't have to feedback everything, as they may prefer to keep some of the things they have talked about to themselves rather than share them with others.

Meditation and Prayer

Each session ends with ten minutes of readings, meditation and prayer. Ask for four volunteers to read the readings and the closing prayer. Never impose a reading on someone and only read yourself if there are no volunteers.

After the Course

Encourage participants to go to church as often as they can in Holy Week, especially on Palm Sunday, Maundy Thursday and Good Friday. It may be possible to link some of the course material/themes to these services.

Consider keeping the group going when the course has ended, after a suitable break, to continue meeting regularly for Bible study, prayer and fellowship. It may be a good idea to sound people out about this in the final group session. If participants have enjoyed the course and bonded well together you may be surprised at how many will want to go on meeting together in this way in the future.

Chapter Two

St James "the Great" and Santiago de Compostela

James, son of Zebedee, was a Galilean fisherman who, with his brother John, was one of the first disciples called by Jesus to follow him. He is patron saint of Spain and pilgrims, and his Feast Day is celebrated in the Western Church on 25 July. He is called James "the Great" to distinguish him from the other apostle James, son of Alphaeus, who is known as James "the Less". (There is also another James, James "the Just", the brother of Jesus, who became the leader of the church in Jerusalem and to whom the authorship of The Letter of James is traditionally attributed.) James is the English rendering of *Iakobos* in New Testament Greek, itself derived from the Hebrew name *Ya'aqov* (Jacob), "the supplanter".

James and John, along with Peter, formed an inner circle of three among the twelve. They alone were present at the raising of Jairus' daughter (Mark 5.37), the Transfiguration (Mark 9.2) and the agony in Gethsemane (Mark 14.33). Jesus gave James and John the nickname "Boanerges, that is, Sons of Thunder" (Mark 3.17), possibly on account of their fiery temper. They were rebuked by Jesus for offering to command fire to come down from heaven to consume a Samaritan village that had refused to receive Jesus (Luke 9.54). They also caused anger among the other disciples when they requested a place of honour in Christ's kingdom, sitting one at his right hand and one at his left (Mark 10.37); Jesus replied that their request was not his to grant, but the cup of suffering he was to drink they also would drink. This prophecy was fulfilled for James when he was beheaded on the order of Herod Agrippa I (Acts 12.2), believed to be in the year AD 44. He is the only apostle whose martyrdom is recorded in the New Testament, and James is thus believed to be the first of the twelve to be martyred for his faith.

What follows is James' story so far as it can be ascertained from the New Testament, and the story of how the few known facts about his life grew into a legend. It is also the story of the Way of St James and the city of Santiago de Compostela, "a monument to a legend" (Mullins 2001:209).

St James the Apostle

The Sea of Galilee is an inland freshwater lake, fed from the north by the River Jordan, about thirteen miles long and eight miles wide. Its Hebrew name, *Kinneret*, comes from the word for "harp", which is the shape of the lake. In the gospels it is called by various other names: "the lake of Gennesaret" (Luke 5.1), from the name of a nearby Canaanite city, and "the Sea of Tiberias" (John 6.1), from the main harbour of the Sea of Galilee in the port city of Tiberias. Fish was a staple food in first-century Palestine and a thriving fishing industry flourished on the Sea of Galilee as it does to this day. Carp, catfish and tilapia ("St Peter's fish") abound.

As Jesus walked by the Sea of Galilee, he saw James and John with their father Zebedee in their boat mending their nets. Jesus called them and immediately they left their boat and their father and followed him (Matthew 4.21-22). Like Simon and Andrew just moments before them, their response to Jesus' call was immediate. It was a call from God and it was the beginning of the messianic community – the Church. All the initiative is with Jesus: he comes to them, they do not come to him; he sees them, they do not see him; he speaks to them, they do not speak to him. The story mirrors Elijah's call of Elisha to be his disciple (1 Kings 19.19-21) and God's call of prophets in general (e.g. Amos 7.15), who are uprooted from their ordinary existence as ploughman or herdsman to prophesy to God's people Israel. Here, humble fishermen are called as disciples to participate in the divine mission to humanity – to "fish for people" (Matthew 4.19), to gather men and women for the kingdom.

Without a word, James and John leave their nets and follow Jesus, abandoning not only their livelihoods but also their father. They have never seen Jesus before; they have seen no miracles nor heard any of his teachings. No explanation has been given to them as to why they should follow Jesus, what following him will mean, or where the journey will lead them. In Luke's account, however, the call of the fishermen takes place immediately after a miraculous catch of fish (Luke 5.1-11), "a psychologically plausible account of why they left everything to follow Jesus" (Culpepper 1995:116).

It is likely that the setting for these encounters is Capernaum, a settlement that stretched along the lakefront. Simon and Andrew had a house there (Mark 1.29), and Simon, James and John were partners in the same fishing enterprise (Luke 5.10). Accordingly, they are pictured as wealthy enough to own houses, to own or lease boats, and to employ hired hands (Mark 1.20). As such, they probably had some education and would have been regarded as relatively prosperous in their local community. "The idea that they were impoverished, persons on the margins of society is unlikely" (Perkins 1995:540).

James, along with the other disciples, followed Jesus around Galilee and Judea for the whole of his earthly ministry – one year according to the synoptic gospels or three years according to the Fourth Gospel – and eventually came to the final week in Jerusalem. On the Thursday, having eaten the Passover meal together, they went with Jesus to the Garden of Gethsemane where Jesus took Peter, James and John to pray with him away from the others, only for them to fall asleep (Mark 14.37). And then, following his betrayal and arrest, "all the disciples deserted him and fled" (Matthew 26.56).

It was not James' finest hour and we do not hear of him again until after the resurrection. In stark contrast, Matthew records that James' mother witnessed the crucifixion (Matthew 27.56), along with many other women who had followed Jesus from Galilee and provided for him out of their means. Mark names James' mother as "Salome" (Mark 15.40), but "[Matthew's] description of her as 'the mother of the sons of Zebedee' reminds the reader of the absence of Jesus' disciples and the presence of the women as their substitutes" (Boring 1995:493). They are still present after all the male disciples have fled; they will be the ones who are able to validate Jesus' death and burial and serve as witnesses to the empty tomb, and their testimony to what happened is critical to understanding the authenticity of Jesus' death and resurrection. (If Salome is the same person as "[Jesus'] mother's sister" recorded in John 19.25, as some commentators believe, then James was a first cousin of Jesus on his mother's side.)

James and all the other apostles saw the risen Lord. Matthew records the commissioning of the eleven on a mountain in Galilee (Matthew 28.16-20), and Luke the appearance of Jesus to the eleven in Jerusalem on the evening of the first Easter (Luke 24.36-49). John records the same appearance in Jerusalem (John 20.19-23), followed by a second a week later (John 20.26-29). And then, in what is reckoned by scholarly consensus to be a postscript to the Fourth Gospel, added at a later date either by the Evangelist himself or by another member of the same Christian community, the author narrates an appearance of Jesus to the disciples by the Sea of Galilee. "The sons of Zebedee", listed among the seven disciples present, are mentioned here for the first and only time in the Fourth Gospel (John 21.2). Here, the author recounts a miraculous catch of fish, strikingly similar to the episode in Luke 5, which is hauled ashore in the net. The disciples now join Jesus in drawing people to God, marking the extension of Jesus' work into the disciples' work. "This story thus stands as the narrative fulfillment of Jesus' promises to his disciples in the Farewell

Discourse that they will share in his works" (O'Day 1995:858).

Luke records that the eleven witnessed the Ascension of Jesus from the Mount of Olives (Luke 24.50-51, Acts 1.9) before returning to Jerusalem where, with the newly chosen Matthias, they were all together in one place for the coming of the Holy Spirit at Pentecost (Acts 2.1-4). The Acts of the Apostles contains many stories about the life and work of the early Church, although its title is something of a misnomer since few of the apostles chosen by Jesus are actually prominent. The notable exceptions are Peter and John, who were "acknowledged pillars" of the Jerusalem church (Galatians 2.9). The most prominent figure is Paul, who is not an apostle by Luke's definition (Acts 1.21-22), and we are introduced to many of Paul's companions and co-workers such as Barnabas, Silas and Timothy. James the Great is not mentioned at all by name from the moment he returns to Jerusalem from the Mount of Olives after the Ascension (Acts 1.13) until his death, when Herod Agrippa I, grandson of Herod the Great and ruler of Palestine from AD 41-44, had him "killed with the sword" (Acts 12.2), the first of the apostles to drink the chalice of the Lord. If we accept the traditional date of James' death as AD 44 and the most widely held date of the crucifixion as AD 33, this gives a period of eleven years in which his whereabouts are largely unaccounted for, allowing plenty of scope for a legend to be born.

The Galician Legend

With many variations the story goes that St James (in Spanish *Santiago*), responding to Christ's command to "make disciples of all nations" (Matthew 28.19), travelled to Spain to spread the gospel, a missionary endeavour that met with little success. On 2 January in the year AD 40, the Blessed Virgin Mary appeared to him in a miraculous apparition beside the Ebro River at Caesar Augustus (today called Zaragoza) in northeast Spain. She appeared on a pillar, the one to which Jesus had been tied for his flagellation, and revived his spirits. On this spot James built the first church ever to be dedicated to Mary, now the site of the present Basilica of Our Lady of the Pillar. Shortly afterwards he returned to Jerusalem where he was beheaded.

Immediately after his execution, his body (with its head) was taken by his followers back to Spain by ship, sailing from the port of Jaffa on the Mediterranean coast to the Bay of Padrón in the region of Galicia in northwest Spain. Upon their arrival they were arrested by the authorities and thrown into gaol, only to be released by an angel. The local ruler of the district, Queen Lupa, ordered the body of James to be buried on a hillside where there lived a renowned snake that would be sure to finish off these troublesome foreigners for good. But, on seeing the sign of the cross, the snake died, and Queen Lupa immediately converted to Christianity. She allowed the body of James to be given a proper burial in a tomb, in which two of his disciples were also later buried.

Can any of this really be true? In Paul's Letter to the Romans, probably written around AD 57, Paul announces his intention to set out on a missionary journey to Spain (Romans 15.22-29). He specifically makes it his ambition to proclaim the gospel "not where Christ has already been named, so that I do not build on someone else's foundation" (Romans 15.20). This suggests that Paul knew of no previous Christian mission to Spain. If Spain had already been evangelised by James, it seems highly unlikely that Paul would ever have gone there; there were fresh territories to be evangelised and churches he had already established to be revisited. Indeed, church literature for the next 350 years is entirely silent on any connection between James and Spain. So how, then, did the legend emerge?

A vague comment was made by St Jerome in about the year 400, when he wrote that James *and* John, after they had been called by Jesus, were "changed from fishers of fish into fishers of men, and they preached the gospel from Jerusalem to Illyria [east coast of the Adriatic Sea] and Spain." The first explicit reference that James took the gospel to Spain appeared in the *Breviarium Apostolorum*, a seventh-century Latin translation and interpolation of an earlier Greek text listing the mission fields of the apostles (which did not put James in Spain). This claim that James was responsible for evangelising Spain – but not that he was buried there – was then repeated in other texts throughout the Latin Church. These testimonies based on the *Breviarium* include one from St Aldhelm, Abbot of Malmesbury and first Bishop of Sherborne (d. 709). In 711 the Moors invaded Spain and usurped power from the Visigoths; a Christian champion was needed to help defend Spain against Islam, and James seemed the obvious candidate.

Following earlier Greek texts, the *Breviarium* recorded that James' body was buried in Achaia (or Anchaion) Marmarica. The precise location is unclear, but Marmarica was an area of North Africa corresponding to what is now the border region between Egypt and Libya. Why (or when) James' body was taken there for burial is not known, but in terms of its proximity to Judea and the existence of the Coptic Church in Egypt from the fifth century it is at least a feasible proposition. Once again, however, something appears to have got lost in translation, for by the ninth century *in Achaia Marmarica* had, in certain Latin texts, become *in arca marmorica*, "in a marble tomb". This meant that the bones of the saint could be anywhere. Soon after the crowning of Charlemagne as Holy Roman Emperor (and chief defender of Christianity against the Infidel) by Pope Leo III in the year 800, the tomb of the apostle James was apparently discovered in Spain's "western extremities". An addition made in 838 to a history of Christian martyrs by Florus de Lyon records the find, and a later martyrology by Usuard of St-Germain-des-Prés (c. 865) repeats the claim. Neither, however, specifies the precise location.

Documents dating from the eleventh century fill in the details of the "discovery" of the tomb. According to these texts, in the year 813 a Christian hermit by the name of Pelayo had a vision, in which angelic voices revealed to him the whereabouts of the tomb by means of a cluster of stars. He immediately informed Theodomir, the local bishop of the port city of Iria Flavia (d. 847), and in dense woodland on Mount Libredón, some twelve miles from the seat of the bishop, a marble tomb was duly discovered. In the tomb were three bodies, which the bishop immediately pronounced to be the remains of St James and two of his disciples who had brought his body to Spain. King Alfonso II, king of the northern kingdom of the Asturias (d. 842), visited the tomb and declared that James was henceforth to be regarded as patron saint and protector of Spain. He built a small chapel over the tomb and a monastery nearby, and the town that grew up around these sites in the ninth century became known as *Campus Stellae*, "Field of Stars", later shortened to Compostela.

Modern scholarship suggests that the name Compostela actually originates from the Latin word *compostum* meaning "burial ground", and recent excavations beneath the present cathedral at Santiago have uncovered evidence of a Roman cemetery and a pre-Roman necropolis. Nevertheless, the legend that the apostle's bones had been discovered in the early ninth century at Santiago de Compostela was, by the eleventh century, already firmly established, and the precise details of the find probably didn't matter very much. But why was the apparent discovery made here, in this particular part of Spain close to Iria Flavia and the Bay of Padrón? Evidence exists of a cult of relic worshippers located at Mérida in southwest Spain as early as the year 600, who fled to Galicia a century later to escape the conquering Moors, apparently knowing that a similar religious group already existed at Iria Flavia. The supposition is that their flight by sea up the Atlantic coast to the Bay of Padrón later became the basis of the legend that James' body itself had been brought to Spain in this way.

From the mid-ninth century onwards, Spain was gradually being re-conquered by the Christians, working first from the Asturias and then the new kingdoms of León, Navarre, Castile and Aragon. In 1492, King Ferdinand V and Queen Isabella I completed the re-conquest of Spain by driving the Moors from their last stronghold in Granada. St James had certainly proved his worth as the champion of Christianity that Spain had sought seven centuries earlier. He was *Santiago Matamoros*, "St James the Moor-slayer", and is said to have appeared on several occasions in the thick of battle, personally routing and slaughtering the armies of Muhammad. He was the *miles Christi* or "soldier of Christ", and is pictured in churches along the pilgrim road as the soldier apostle astride a white charger, sword in hand, slaying the Infidel beneath his feet.

By the sixteenth century a whole succession of holy relics purporting to relate to St James and other saints and martyrs were being discovered. One such discovery was a series of finds made in a cave in the Sacromonte ("Sacred Mountain") in the Granada district of southern Spain, beginning with a sealed box containing a bone of St Stephen, the first Christian martyr, and part of the cloth used by the Virgin Mary at the crucifixion to dry her tears. The last and greatest find consisted of eighteen books enclosed in lead, the so-called "lead-books of the Sacromonte", supposedly written by someone who had travelled with James to Spain and remained there after the apostle's return to Jerusalem. An official Council authenticated them in 1600, only for Pope Innocent XI to subsequently pronounce them forgeries in 1682.

In the post-Reformation era, Santiago de Compostela naturally held little appeal to Protestant Europe, and was seen by some to represent much of what was wrong with Roman Catholicism. In 1589, the year after the Armada, Queen Elizabeth I sent an army of 14,000 to Galicia to destroy it – a mission that thankfully failed. The English attacked again repeatedly from

1700-1720, during which time the relics of the apostle were hidden away for protection in the wall behind the high altar of the cathedral. In 1878, excavations to retrieve them were undertaken, and what was found was a coffer containing the assorted bones of three men. However, after the skeletons had been reassembled, no one could be quite sure which one was the body of the apostle! Spain held her breath, until it was found that a tiny fragment of James' skull, a revered relic of the cathedral at Pistoia in Tuscany, was found to fit exactly one of the three ancient skulls. In 1884, Pope Leo XIII issued a bull, *Omnipotens Deus*, which verified the identity of the three bodies as being those of St James and his two disciples, Theodosius and Athanasius. Today, the apostle's skull is also claimed to be entombed in the Armenian Cathedral of St James in Jerusalem, and his body in the church of St-Sernin in Toulouse, a gift from the Emperor Charlemagne along with no fewer than five other apostles!

The Way of St James

As soon as news spread of the discovery of the tomb in the early ninth century, pilgrims from all over Europe began to make the long walk to Santiago de Compostela. It started as a trickle, but by the mid-tenth century the pilgrimage was already well established and monasteries along the Way began providing food and shelter for the influx of pilgrims. Perhaps as many as half a million people a year were making the journey at the height of its popularity in the eleventh and twelfth centuries. After all, these remains could hardly be more important in the hierarchy of saintly relics. The saints closest in time and place to Jesus held the greatest degree of sanctity, and so an apostle who was a member of the inner circle of three – and also the first apostle to be martyred – was clearly very high up on the list indeed. In the Middle Ages, the pilgrimage to Jerusalem was the first in importance, and then the pilgrimage to Rome to the tombs of St Peter and St Paul. Although the pilgrimage to Santiago de Compostela was third in importance, by the late Middle Ages it had become the most popular of the trio of so-called "great pilgrimages". As regards the tradition of pilgrimage on foot, it is the only one that survives today.

Four main pilgrim routes passed through France on the way to Spain. One of these began in Paris, where pilgrims from all over northern Europe gathered on the Right Bank at the Place St-Jacques, the Square of St James. The last thing they did before setting off was to attend mass in the Church of St-Jacques-de-la-Boucherie, before making their way up the Rue St-Jacques, out of the city through the Porte St-Jacques, and on to the open road south towards Étampes.

It was a hazardous two-month journey, undertaken as an act of piety arising out of a true sense of religious devotion and a desire to venerate holy relics. But not everyone undertook the journey of their own free will, and to understand properly the spirit of medieval pilgrimage it is necessary to understand also the sacrament of penance. The Roman Church was preoccupied with the saving of souls through *remissio peccatorum*, the remission (or forgiveness) of sins. Repentance and confession were not of themselves enough to ensure remission; it was necessary also for the penitent sinner to perform certain acts prescribed by the priest in order to receive absolution. One such act of penance was to undertake a pilgrimage: not only would the suffering involved serve as atonement but also the penitent would have the benefit of contact with the relics of the saints, to whom he could pray that they might intercede with the Almighty on his behalf. Undertaken in this spirit, the medieval pilgrimage was a passport to heaven and the pilgrim routes themselves were the roads to heaven.

Unless, that is, you were rich enough to line the coffers of the church! By the late Middle Ages the wealthy could obtain the easier option of making a payment instead, the amount being determined by a fixed scale of payment to each shrine based on the distance and hardship involved in getting there. A number of these so-called "redemption tables" have survived, so it is known, for example, that the cost of avoiding a pilgrimage from Flanders either to Santiago or Rome was £12. Whereas before you had to earn your place in heaven, now you could simply buy it.

It was also a way of acquiring "indulgences" for oneself or for a loved one – each indulgence annulling a certain number of sins or reducing the time a sinner would have to spend in purgatory. In 1456, the pilgrimage to Santiago would have earned you remission of one-third of your sins; if you died en route, total remission; for hearing mass in the cathedral, 200 days off purgatory. Santiago was a prime source of pardons, and a certificate called the *Compostelana* was issued to pilgrims as proof that they had actually completed the pilgrimage and received their indulgences. Once again, by the late Middle Ages the Roman Church was selling indulgences, a scandal that in no small part led to the European Reformations.

The cult of relics itself was a moneymaker for the medieval Church; in an age of superstition they were seen to have potency and magic power, and to possess relics was to ensure a constant stream of the sick and the sinful to your door. They, of course, would have to pay for the honour of offering up prayers, and a whole pilgrimage industry grew up around the cult of relics. The more important the saint the bigger the reward, and the Cathedral of St James at Santiago de Compostela grew immensely rich, a treasure chest swelled further by gifts from rulers and taxes on the people paid in thanksgiving to the apostle for his part in their liberation from Moorish rule.

The pilgrimage to Santiago became such a popular devotion that St James became the patron saint of pilgrims, *Santiago Peregrino*. James' symbol is three gold scallop shells on a blue field, and so it was that the scallop shell became the badge of pilgrims travelling to and from Santiago. How James himself acquired the scallop insignia is not entirely clear. The scallop was first a symbol of Venus, the Roman goddess of love, who legend relates was born in a shell and carried across the sea to the Greek island of Cythera. She is identified with the Greek goddess Aphrodite, born of the sea foam and goddess of seafarers. The scallop emblem appears as a symbol of love in early Coptic churches dating from the fifth century, and the first basilica at Santiago (899) was of Coptic design. The symbol may well have travelled with the design, and an obvious connection can be made between the scallop shell and the apostle who first took the love of Christ to Spain and whose body was later carried across the sea to the Bay of Padrón.

Scallops happen to be common on the Galician coast and it is here that for many the journey ends, not at Santiago de Compostela. Having reached the end of the Way at Santiago, many pilgrims are drawn to walk a few days more, either to the Bay of Padrón or further still to the most westerly point of Galicia, Cape Finisterre, "the end of the earth". Here ends the "Way of the Stars" or "Milky Way", a prehistoric route across northern Spain from the Mediterranean to the Atlantic and a possible source for the legend of the "Field of Stars".

Scallops also feature in a number of stories concerning James' miraculous powers. One involves a knight who was saved from drowning by the apostle, who emerged from the sea covered in scallop shells. Another tells of a widow whose husband had drowned at sea; she prayed to James, whereupon her husband rose from his watery grave covered in scallop shells. Whatever its origin in connection to St James, by the twelfth century the scallop shell had become firmly established as the insignia of pilgrims – a badge of privilege and protection and a ticket to free board and lodging. Today it is seen everywhere, on churches and way markers, in guide books and the pilgrim's *credencial* or "passport", and it is the must have souvenir of all who have travelled the Way.

From the Pyrenees, "the long road to heaven" passes through more than 350 towns and villages before finally reaching "the heavenly city" (Hebrews 11.16) of Santiago de Compostela, a symbol of "the holy city, the new Jerusalem" (Revelation 21.2) and of the culmination of the pilgrim's life and union with God. Here it was that Alfonso II had first built a small chapel over the tomb of the apostle. This was quickly replaced by a larger church in around 830-40, and then by a basilica in 899 on the order of Alfonso III. This was destroyed by the Moorish commander Al-Mansur in 997, and another erected in 1003. Its rebuilding into a cathedral began in 1075 under the supervision of Bishop Diego Peláez. It was finished and consecrated in 1211.

The original plain, simple Romanesque cathedral is barely recognisable today. Major alterations and additions were begun during the fifteenth century, when the cupola that caps the crossing of the transept and nave was completed. In the sixteenth century, the cloisters were added and the towers constructed. In the seventeenth century, much of the exterior of the cathedral was embellished in the Baroque style and a bell tower built. In the eighteenth century, the Baroque façade that today dominates the entire external appearance of the cathedral was added, and the open space at the west front of the cathedral, the Plaza del Obradoiro, was created. Here was where the *obradoiro* (workshop) once stood, where the stone for the façade was cut and carved.

The majestic western entrance to the nave, the Pórtico de la Gloria, is of such richness and complexity that it is held to be one of the outstanding achievements of medieval sculpture anywhere in the world. The Pórtico, with its two hundred superbly carved figures, was created by a Frenchman known as Maestro Mateo, who was master builder at Santiago from 1165 to the time of the cathedral's consecration in 1211. It is enclosed within a narthex (or porch) inside the Baroque-style exterior of the cathedral and is composed of three carved arches, the central arch being the entrance to the nave. Dividing the central arch is a pillar, above which is a sculpture of St James seated serenely above an elaborately carved Jesse Tree, receiving pilgrims at their journey's end and bidding them enter. Welcoming them in the name of the Lord, he holds a pilgrim's staff in the form of a tau cross, a symbol of redemption and the completion of the pilgrimage of life. For centuries it has been a tradition for pilgrims entering the cathedral to insert their fingers between the twisted stems of the tree, and today, after eight hundred years, five finger holes are worn deep into the marble.

Inside the cathedral, the supposed relics of the apostle and his two disciples, Theodosius and Athanasius, are contained in a nineteenth-century silver reliquary in a crypt to which visitors descend behind the high altar. Equally important to the pilgrim is the huge Baroque statue of the apostle, which is raised high above the altar and acts as the focal point within the entire cathedral. The statue can be reached by means of some stairs mounting left and right behind the altar, allowing it to be embraced by all who approach it.

The famous *botafumeiro* ("smoke belcher") is the huge censer suspended from beneath the cupola. Controlled by eight men on the end of ropes, it is swung the entire length of the transept – from just above head height to the uppermost point of the vault – to disperse the smoke of the incense and perfume the pilgrims. Today, viewed in its entirety, this gigantic cruciform cathedral, 98 metres long and 67 metres wide, is unquestionably one of the most magnificent cathedrals in the world. Like the legend of St James itself – of monstrous proportions and exaggerated by centuries of embellishment and overwhelming decoration – the cathedral stands as a fitting monument to the tale. It is perhaps one of the most extraordinary stories ever told: "Honed over centuries of discoveries, interpretations, claims, and counterclaims, it lies somewhere between legend and fact, between superstition and belief" (Gitlitz and Davidson 2000:XIII).

Chapter Three

The Course

Week One: What are We Saved from?

In those days Jesus came from Nazareth of Galilee and was baptized by John in the Jordan. And just as he was coming up out of the water, he saw the heavens torn apart and the Spirit descending like a dove on him. And a voice came from heaven, "You are my Son, the Beloved; with you I am well pleased." (Mark 1.9-11, *Lent 1, Year B*)

Prelude

Our Lenten journey begins in the wilderness by the River Jordan, the great river across which Joshua led the Israelites into the Promised Land of Canaan. The river's source is far to the north on Mount Hermon, on the border between Syria and Lebanon, where streams carry melting snowfalls from the peaks above. The river flows southwards through the Sea of Galilee and on to its end at the Dead Sea. The traditional site of Jesus' baptism is located near the Monastery of St Jerasimos, maintained by the Orthodox Church, one of twenty monasteries founded in the Judean desert during the Byzantine period. Many pilgrims today are baptised in the Jordan River here and at other sites elsewhere.

John the Baptist occupies a pivotal position in the Christian Bible as the last of the Old Testament prophets and the first of the New Testament saints. He proclaimed "a baptism of repentance for the forgiveness of sins" (Mark 1.4), calling on Jews to confess their sins in readiness for the coming of Jesus. John was sent by God to prepare a way in the wilderness, "the way of the Lord" (Mark 1.3), a prophetic cry that once heralded the imminent return of the Jews from their long exile in Babylon (Isaiah 40.3).

The cry still carried its note of triumph as it now announced the imminent arrival of the Messiah to lead his people out of their Old World captivity into a new age, a time when the Holy Spirit would be poured out on all people (Joel 2.28).

John's call for national repentance was accompanied by a call to baptism (from the Greek *baptizein* meaning "to dip"), a symbolic washing or cleansing in water. It was a ritual that accords with the many other Jewish rites of purification and recalls Israel's passing through the waters of the Red Sea to new life in the Promised Land. John called upon all Jews to repent and be baptised, to be cleansed from their sins (Psalm 51.2), "for the kingdom of heaven has come near" (Matthew 3.2). The baptism that he offered was a sign of that repentance, a public witness to a new start. Despite John's unwillingness, Jesus insisted on being baptised too. It seems anomalous that Jesus, who was without sin (Hebrews 4.15, 1 John 3.5), should submit to John in this manner, but Jesus answered him, "it is proper for us in this way to fulfill all righteousness" (Matthew 3.15). His baptism was the recapitulation of the birth of Israel in the Red Sea.

Saved from sin

The substance of God's liberating promise of salvation is the forgiveness of sins. Forgiveness of sins characterises the Christian participation in salvation, for salvation stems from forgiveness. Zechariah's inspired prophecy (traditionally called the *Benedictus*) makes the point clear:

> And you, child, will be called the prophet of the Most High; for you will go before the Lord to prepare his ways, to give knowledge of salvation to his people by the forgiveness of their sins. (Luke 1.76-77)

Even though Jesus himself probably never baptised anyone (John 4.2), forgiveness of sins – and its issue salvation – was, for the ancient Church, intimately connected to the sacrament of baptism.

Baptism signalled new birth through water and the Holy Spirit, an image of new life that we shall explore further next week. It also united the baptised with Christ in his death, burial and resurrection (Romans 6.3-4): in baptism we die to our sinful life, rising again from the water to a new life in Christ. After Peter's Pentecost speech, which marks the beginning of Christian witness to the saving work of God in Christ, his hearers ask how they should respond and Peter replies, "Repent, and be baptised every one of you in the name of Jesus Christ so that your sins may be forgiven; and you will receive the gift of the Holy Spirit" (Acts 2.38).

The early Christian view was that forgiveness of sins is something given to us once and for all. It follows that baptism is also something that takes place once and for all, which is what we affirm in the Nicene Creed when we say, "We acknowledge one baptism for the forgiveness of sins." In the early Church, this led to baptism being put off until as late as possible in a person's life so as to lessen the danger of a relapse into sin for which there could be no forgiveness. From the early Middle Ages onwards, however, the practice of infant baptism meant that forgiveness of sins became detached from its connection to baptism. Instead, repeated repentance and forgiveness within the framework of confession became the normal practice in Christian life.

In the context of a contemporary and pluralistic understanding of salvation, we need to ask the question: is it really necessary to be baptised to be saved? The answer is probably not, and here we can take a lead from the Orthodox Bishop Kallistos Ware who writes, "Certainly God is able to save those who have never been baptized" (Ware 1995:109). This allows us to shift our focus onto *Jesus* as Saviour rather than the water of baptism. Jesus Christ, Son of God, is our Saviour, and the distinctiveness of the Christian understanding of salvation is that it is grounded in the life, death and resurrection of Jesus. His very name – *Iēsous* in Greek – is derived from the Hebrew *Y'hosua* (Joshua) meaning "God saves".

The Fourth Gospel records that when John the Baptist saw Jesus coming towards him he declared, "Here is the Lamb of God who takes away the sin of the world!" (John 1.29). The "Lamb of God" recalls the Passover lamb, a lamb "without blemish" (Exodus 12.5) and the symbol of Israel's deliverance in the exodus, tens of thousands of which would be slaughtered every year on the day of Preparation for the Passover. This was the day, according to the Fourth Gospel, when Jesus hung on the cross (John 19.14).

Note John's use of the singular word "sin", which emphasises the world's collective brokenness rather than individual human sins. This does not, however, let us off the hook individually and allow us to be complacent; we cannot ignore the truth that we are born into a world of accumulated wrong-doing to which we add by our own accumulation of wrongs. Nevertheless, the meaning of "sin" in a Christian context is not primarily about individual human faults; rather it is about the wrong foundation of the entire human existence. Sin means ignoring God in the world that God has made. We think we can "go it alone" without God, which is exactly what Adam and Eve did in the mythical story of Genesis 3. The "original sin" was pride, which is why Jesus displays in his life and death the very opposite of pride – humility and total dependence upon God. Sin is what separates us from God; it is above all a divine-human relational problem. Wolfhart Pannenberg, one of the German theological giants of the last century, describes it like this:

> Sin means going astray, failing to find the source of life in our search for life. The going astray consists in every man's striving for the fulfilment of life through enrichment of his own ego, separated from others and from God. (Pannenberg 1972:164)

Forgiveness is the act through which God restores the relationship between himself and sinful humanity: "God was in Christ reconciling the world to himself, not counting their trespasses against them" (2 Corinthians 5.19). Where sin is pardoned, brokenness is made whole.

Saved from evil

If salvation means liberation from sin, which separates us from God, it must have something to do also with being freed from "evil", which is whatever hinders the realisation of good and a person's response to God's saving grace. It is a tradition for Christians to pray for deliverance from evil, and the petition in the Lord's Prayer is an obvious example of this. Evil is manifested in society in such things as racism and other forms of discrimination, and is experienced by individuals who are personally afflicted by evil. The human condition is insecure and vulnerable, threatened from without and within by dark, destructive forces from which we need to be released. We can give these opponents names: loneliness, meaninglessness, guilt, bereavement, illness, exploitation, oppression, unemployment, poverty, debt, addiction, violence and abuse. These are our "demons", real "enemies" that keep us from living a fulfilled and free life and from which God wants to deliver us. Salvation, therefore, has much to do with our *present* life, with the here-and-now, and is not simply concerned with being freed from death for eternal life in the world to come. Salvation happens *now*.

The word salvation has the same root as "salve", a soothing and healing balm. It implies health and wholeness of being, essential soundness and completeness. The saved life is the fully human life, restored to its true condition and right relationship with God. For the Hebrew slaves, salvation was all about their life in this world. Dietrich Bonhoeffer, another of the German theological giants of the last century, writes, "Israel is delivered out of Egypt so that it may live before God as God's people on earth" (Bonhoeffer 2001:124). Salvation exists on this side of death. To be human at all is to be involved in pain and loss, to lead a precarious and even perilous existence, but, as Bonhoeffer says, "Christ takes hold of a man at the centre of his life" (Ibid:124).

God has freed his people in the past and he will do it again; God saves and will go on saving. The challenge for each of us is to recognise the God *who is* (Revelation 1.4). We can seek to understand the God *who was,* and we can look forward with hope to the God *who is to come.* But we need to be most acutely aware that salvation has utmost relevance to the life lived in this world; it is about becoming more fully human and being restored to the fullness of God's image in which we were created. God is present and active in the world today, lives are changed now, and wherever wholeness and healing occur we need to recognise that as being God's liberating and saving work.

The characters we meet in the film *The Way* are all seeking release from one thing or another. They carry their own private struggles on a transcendent journey, a spiritual journey of trans-formation, self-discovery and enlightenment.

The Characters in *The Way*

Tom – A wealthy Californian ophthalmologist, already widowed, now mourning the sudden and tragic loss of his only son Daniel who died on the Camino.

Joost – A jovial, food-loving Dutchman, trapped in a loveless marriage.

Sarah – A bitter Canadian divorcee, previously married to a physically abusive husband, who underwent an abortion because she feared he would harm their baby as well.

Jack – A garrulous Irish travel writer with writer's block, who has given up on God because of all the damage the Church and religion have caused in his own country.

None of these characters sets out to walk the Camino for religious reasons. None is on a journey to find God – but God finds them! Each has a life-changing encounter with "the way" himself (John 14.6).

Saved from death

If, as we established earlier, sin is what separates us from God, then the forgiveness of sin through the cross of Jesus gives us warrant to hope even beyond death for eternal life with God. We have also thought about the many evils that afflict us as "enemies" from which God wants to deliver us, and Paul refers to death as "the last enemy to be destroyed" (1 Corinthians 15.26). The coming resurrection of the dead at the end of history is clearly understood by Paul to mean entry into a wholly new kind of life beyond the power of death, and it is the mortal, crucified and risen Christ who is Paul's model for our death and resurrection: "For since we believe that Jesus died and rose again, even so, through Jesus, God will bring with him those who have died" (1 Thessalonians 4.14).

The Christian resurrection hope is faith firmly rooted in the God who raised Jesus from the dead, thereby pledging to raise also those who believe in Jesus. His resurrection is not merely a wondrous event that confirms him as the Son of God; rather it is the beginning – "the first fruits" (1 Corinthians 15.20) – of a much greater harvest of which we are to be part. What God has sown is not in vain; all will bear fruit – miraculous fruit – in the life of the world to come. God has acted and will act again in ways beyond our experience and our comprehension. We are called to stretch our understanding and to imagine life unlike anything we now know, but it is God's promise of triumph over death:

Death has been swallowed up in victory.
Where, O death, is your victory?

Where, O death, is your sting?
(1 Corinthians 15.54-55)

The image is one of a reversal of death and of the dead entering into a wholly new kind of life beyond the power of death.

Christianity is above all a tradition characterised by hope, a hope not of an extension of the present order of things but of the transforming work of God who will "make all things new" (Revelation 21.5) – a new heaven and a new earth. This is the kingdom of God that will come upon us in the great renewal of all things, a totally renewed creation marked by the personal presence of Jesus himself. This new creation is not the *replacement* of the present creation but its *renewal*, the eternal future of the present world in which we live. And so nothing of this world will be lost; everything of value in God's good and present creation, all that God himself loves and treasures, will not disappear into nothingness but will be transformed into something new and better and gathered into God's eternal future. All this – and more – is grounded in the life, death and resurrection of the Father's Beloved Son, whose earthly ministry was prefaced by that of John the Baptist in the wilderness of Judea.

Group Session

0.00   Leader
Welcome the group, introduce yourself, and run through any housekeeping points. Check that everyone has a copy of this book. Ask each member of the group to say a few words about themselves: their name, where they live, what they do, and what their particular ministry is in their local church (e.g. mowing the churchyard, children's leader, sacristan, or baking cakes for church fundraising events). Check that each member of the group has read and agrees to the "Rules of Engagement". **10 minutes**

0.10   Film Clip 1

Tom has arrived in St-Jean-Pied-de-Port on the French side of the Pyrenees. He gives instructions for Daniel's body to be cremated and sets out on the Camino carrying the casket of ashes. (Daniel appears in flashback wearing an orange cagoule.) **5 minutes**

0.15   Brainstorm

What did you find interesting or thought-provoking in that clip? What issues or questions does it raise for you? Was there anything you didn't understand and would like to have clarified? **5 minutes**

0.20   Group Discussion

What is Tom's motivation for doing the pilgrimage? Why does Captain Henri say, "You walk the Way only for yourself," and how does he know this? What do you think is the significance of the stone that Henri gives Tom for when he gets to the *Cruz de Ferro* (Iron Cross) and what might this represent for Tom? **10 minutes**

0.30   In Small Groups

How did your faith journey begin? Was there a particular incident in your life that led you to take the first steps? Was there someone in particular who showed you the way? **10 minutes**

0.40   Feedback and Share

Leader: allow each small group to feedback and share with everyone else some of the things they have talked about. **5 minutes**

0.45   Film Clip 2

Here we meet Joost, who Tom has already met briefly in St-Jean before beginning the pilgrimage. **5 minutes**

0.50   Brainstorm
What did you find interesting or thought-provoking in that clip? What issues or questions does it raise for you? Was there anything you didn't understand and would like to have clarified? **5 minutes**

0.55   Group Discussion
What do we learn about Joost from this clip and what do you think of him? How does Tom react to him and how might you have responded differently? If Tom's "enemy" is bereavement, what might be the enemy or enemies from which Joost needs deliverance? **10 minutes**

1.05   In Small Groups
Why is Tom scattering Daniel's cremated remains along the Way? Why do you think some people give instructions for their ashes to be scattered in a place to which they had an attachment in their lifetime, and what might this possibly reveal? Why might others prefer their ashes or the ashes of a loved one to be interred in one place, especially in a churchyard or cemetery? **10 minutes**

1.15   Feedback and Share
Leader: allow each small group to feedback and share with everyone else some of the things they have talked about. **5 minutes**

1.20   Meditation and Prayer

Reader 1

Save me, O God, for the waters have come up to my neck. I sink in deep mire, where there is no foothold; I have come into deep waters, and the flood sweeps over me. I am weary with my crying; my throat is parched. My eyes grow dim with waiting for my God ... Answer me, O LORD, for your steadfast love is good; according to your abundant mercy, turn to me. Do not hide your face from your servant, for I am in distress – make haste to answer me. Draw near to me, redeem me, set me free because of my enemies. (Psalm 69.1-3, 16-18)

Pause

I called to the LORD out of my distress, and he answered me; out of the belly of Sheol I cried, and you heard my voice. You cast me into the deep, into the heart of the seas, and the flood surrounded me; all your waves and your billows passed over me ... I went down to the land whose bars closed upon me forever; yet you brought up my life from the Pit, O LORD my God. (Jonah 2.2-3, 6)

Pause

[Jesus said to the crowd,] "Everything that the Father gives me will come to me, and anyone who comes to me I will never drive away; for I have come down from heaven, not to do my own will, but the will of him who sent me. And this is the will of him who sent me, that I should lose nothing of all that he has given me, but raise it up on the last day. This is indeed the will of my Father, that all who see the Son and believe in him may have eternal life; and I will raise them up on the last day." (John 6.37-40)

One minute's silence for reflection

Reader 2

An extract from *Food for the Fed-Up* by The Reverend G. A. Studdert Kennedy, army chaplain in the First World War, affectionately known as "Woodbine Willie":

I have the vision of the great creative Father with Whom I seek to be at one, and I know that the only possible reason I have for expecting that I can be at one with Him is that there is in me something of the Spirit of Jesus, something of His Divinely perfect humanity. It is not mine, and it is not me, it is a gift from God, a gift which comes to me through His Cross, and through His Saints, through His martyrs, and His Church. The New Life is in me, the Life of Jesus Christ, and because of Him, alive though crucified, in me, I can seek and find forgiveness with God. I know what I mean when I say that I am 'washed in the Blood of the Lamb,' for blood is Life, Life given and outpoured, and it is by the outpouring of the New Life into me that I am saved. It is not merely because He was crucified once and rose again two thousand years ago, but because by that act He is revealed as crucified, yet always rising again in me, that I am being saved, and that I hope at last to be completely saved. I know also what I am saved from; not from any curse of God (an impossible conception), not from any eternal punishment for sin in the world to come, but from sin itself, from selfishness, from meanness, from greed, from the sin which is its own hell. Thus I find the very heart of the Christian Faith and cast away its husk. God is revealed to me in Christ, and I can know Him as He is, and in that growing knowledge find Eternal Life. (Studdert Kennedy 2007:92-93)

One minute's silence for reflection

Reader 3

An extract from *Recovering the Scandal of the Cross* by Joel Green, Dean of the School of Theology at Asbury Theological Seminary in Wilmore, Kentucky, and Mark Baker, Assistant Professor of Theology and Mission at Mennonite Brethren Biblical Seminary in Fresno, California:

> Tragically, many Christians (and former believers) still live in fear of a God who seems so intent on punishing, and much less willing to forgive, than folks we encounter in day-to-day life.
>
> Again, disobedience must be included in any discussion of sin, just as forgiveness is integral to salvation as this is developed in Scripture. We are simply insisting that sin and salvation are larger categories, that they involve more than our most popular atonement images allow.
>
> What is the human condition to which the cross addresses itself? Even to raise the question is to be confronted with the limitations of any answer. We can speak in broad and basic terms about the human situation. At the same time, we must realize that the fundamental, nonnegotiable human need for God is experienced in different ways by different people in different places and at different times. Indeed, in our own lives as Christians, we have come to God with arms open wide with different needs: hope in the midst of despair, direction in the midst of lostness, love in the midst of rejection and so on. If this accurately reflects our autobiographies as Christians, can we not see how different peoples might understand and articulate their life questions in ways that are both like and unlike our own? (Green and Baker 2003:203)

One minute's silence for reflection

Reader 4

O merciful God,
forgive me all the sins that I have committed
against you and against my fellow men.
I trust in your grace

and commit my life wholly into your hands.
Do with me according to your will
and as is best for me.
Whether I live or die, I am with you,
and you, my God, are with me.
Lord, I wait for your salvation
and for your kingdom.
Amen.

(Dietrich Bonhoeffer, "Prayers for Fellow-Prisoners, Christmas 1943", in *Letters and Papers from Prison*)

Week Two: What are We Saved for?

Now there was a Pharisee named Nicodemus, a leader of the Jews. He came to Jesus by night and said to him, "Rabbi, we know that you are a teacher who has come from God; for no one can do these signs that you do apart from the presence of God." Jesus answered him, "Very truly, I tell you, no one can see the kingdom of God without being born from above." (John 3.1-3, *Lent 2, Year A*)

Prelude

If we read the whole of the narrative about Nicodemus' visit to Jesus (John 3.1-21), we discover that Nicodemus is a bold questioner and a challenging debater. Perhaps we can learn something from him, because I think it is fair to say that many of us find it difficult to share our doubts about our faith – or even admit that we have any. But I think it's alright to have doubts and questions and to take these to Jesus just as Nicodemus did, because it is only by expressing these doubts and asking questions that our faith can grow. That's why group study courses in Lent are so valuable, because they provide a forum for those questions to be asked.

Nicodemus, a member of the Sanhedrin (the ruling council of the Jews), seeks out Jesus in Jerusalem under cover of darkness. We have been told at the end of the previous chapter of John that many in Jerusalem who had seen the "signs" (miracles) that Jesus was performing "believed in his name" (John 2.23). But that seems to have been as far as their faith went; their belief had not turned into action and they were still on the outside looking in. Nicodemus may have come as a representative of this group to make some further enquiry. The fact that he came at night suggests that he wanted his interest to remain secret from others for fear of damaging his reputation, but "darkness" is also used metaphorically throughout the Fourth Gospel to represent separation from the presence of God.

Nicodemus' first words to Jesus acknowledge him as "a teacher who has come from God", thereby recognising in him and his signs something of God's work. But Jesus does not respond directly to this affirmation; instead he challenges Nicodemus with a teaching: "No one can see the kingdom of God without being born from above." Only a new birth "of water and Spirit" (v. 5) can bring the blessings of the kingdom of God; new life requires new birth, and baptism is the sign and seal of this new birth. "From above" may also be translated "anew". This double meaning, which is possible only in the Greek, speaks of both a *time* of birth (anew) and a *place* from which this new birth is generated (from above). In the same way, "kingdom of God" has both temporal and spatial dimensions: it evokes both the *time* of God's reign and the *place* of God's realm.

The kingdom of God

This new birth of which Jesus speaks gives us access to God and an end to separation from God. It is a powerful offer of new life with God who loves everything that he has made, and it is what we are saved *for*: fullness of life under the sovereignty of God; fully fit for his purposes.

"The kingdom of God" is properly understood to mean the kingly reign or rule of God. Unfortunately, though quite understandably, many people believe that the kingdom of God is a place – a place where God lives and where people may hope to live with God after they die. Although "kingdom" must, as mentioned above, have a spatial dimension (God must reign somewhere), that realm is not a place removed from this world.

The New Testament asserts that, in Jesus of Nazareth, the Messiah or "anointed one" (in Greek *Christos*) was encountered and God's kingdom (reign) was made manifest. The kingdom (reign) of God for which Israel had hoped and prayed has come to pass in Jesus the Christ. God's rule expressed itself in a new and amazing way: not through obedience to the Mosaic Law but in the life, death and resurrection of Jesus. So when Jesus himself says, "The time is fulfilled, and the kingdom of God is at hand" (Mark 1.15), what he is saying is that the time has come for God's will to be accomplished. What God wants to happen is about to take place – indeed it is already happening. Jesus' miracles demonstrate the truth of his claim: God's will *is* being accomplished in remarkable ways. Demons, diseases and the forces of nature are being vanquished, and this is the "good news" of the gospel. God's reign operates to defeat what is evil and bring about what is good, and so there is a clear association between God's rule and life in the present moment.

Nevertheless, there are also references in the New Testament to the kingdom (reign) of God as being still to come. Some of these references are apocalyptic visions, which stress a distinctly future event. Others may be found in well-known Bible passages such as The Lord's Prayer, in which we pray, "Your kingdom come. Your will be done, on earth as it is in heaven" (Matthew 6.10). It is worth noting here that this verse of the prayer is effectively asking for the same thing twice: God's kingdom (reign) will only come when God's will is done, because God can only truly be said to rule when the things he wants to happen actually take place.

Thus the kingdom appears to be something of a dichotomy: already but not yet, a perpetual tension between being present in some way but still to come in its fullness. It is often said that we are living in an "in between" time, a time between the First Christmas and the Last Judgement when Christ will come again to usher in the kingdom through the new creation, "a new heaven and a new earth" (Revelation 21.1), a kingdom which Jesus first reveals and rules before handing his reign over to the Father (1 Corinthians 15.24). Thus the kingdom both encompasses the everyday workings of life in this world and, at the same time, transcends the totality of this life and appears only at the end of history as the completion or fulfilment of this life. It is present and transforming but its real meaning remains hidden; it is only the final condition of all things that will fully express the rule and will of God.

Heaven

"The kingdom of heaven" is specifically Matthew's alternative way of saying "the kingdom of God", in deference to Jewish piety which had come to regard the name *Yahweh* as too sacred to be pronounced. The words "heaven" and "heavens" – in Jewish thought there were seven heavens – appear many times throughout the Bible to signify the present abode of God and his angels, and the ultimate destination of his saints on earth as the place of perfection. It is language that causes some confusion today, as Tom Wright explains:

> The idea that heaven is a distant place, perhaps up in the sky somewhere, is of course easily recognized as misleading today; most people know that that is not actually what we mean by such language. However, I suspect that a great many influential writers, not least hymn writers, in the last few centuries, have been influenced by some form of Deism, with a God who is somewhat removed from present reality, and so all too easily have written about God's dwelling place as 'way beyond the blue' and so on. (Wright 2006:15)

Deism believes that God created the universe but is unable to intervene in the workings of the universe; that God acted in the past but no longer acts in the present. Deism has no proper place in Christian theology (cf. theism), because Christianity regards the continuing presence and activity of God in the world to be an essential element of belief.

Wright suggests that a proper Christian understanding of "heaven" is not as a place remote from the world but as "God's dimension of present reality" (Ibid:7). Heaven and earth are not distant spheres but actually overlap and interlock; the sacred partakes in the reality itself. God is constantly present in the world he has made, not eternally absent in his own abode. Perhaps Belinda Carlisle came close to the truth when she sang, "Heaven is a place on earth". There is clearly much here that connects with what has already been said about the kingdom of God: present (at least in some way if not in all its fullness), active, powerful and transforming.

No discussion about heaven would be complete without thinking about the question: what happens when we die? If we follow Wright's definition of heaven, we cannot say that when we die we "go to heaven" in the sense that we are literally whisked away to some distant place in the sky. Death-sleep-resurrection is the pattern revealed in the New Testament, where "sleep" might be taken to mean "rest in the peace of Christ" until the day of resurrection. This still raises the question of what is meant by "sleep" or "rest". Christopher Cocksworth discerns three interpretations in the tradition of the Church:

1) *A conscious intermediate state*. This interpretation derives from the Jewish idea of the dead being alive "in Paradise", a royal garden (Eden) in the Hebrew Bible. This is the image pictured by Jesus when he told one of the bandits who was crucified with him, "Today you will be with me in Paradise" (Luke 23.43). Paul tells of an ecstatic experience he had earlier in his life in which he was "caught up into Paradise", which he also calls "the third heaven" (2 Corinthians 12.2-4). Elsewhere, Paul talks about being "away from the body and at home with the Lord" (2 Corinthians 5.8) and of his desire "to depart and be with Christ" (Philippians 1.23).

2) *An unconscious intermediate state*. This interpretation sees death as an unconscious, dreamless sleep, from which we will

be woken at the coming of the Lord: "For the trumpet will sound, and the dead will be raised" (1 Corinthians 15.52). Again Paul writes, "For the Lord himself, with a cry of command, with the archangel's call and with the sound of God's trumpet, will descend from heaven, and the dead in Christ will rise first" (1 Thessalonians 4.16). Martin Luther (1483-1546) seemed to adopt this interpretation of sleep, pointing out that, as far as the individual's perception is concerned, death and resurrection will happen almost instantaneously.

3) *No intermediate state.* This interpretation actually suggests that there is no period between death and resurrection, and that the dead have already been raised to newness of life. God's purposes of salvation have been fulfilled in the instant of death; the dead have stepped out of our time into the eternity of life with God. Cocksworth argues against this idea on the grounds that there can be no resurrection without (or before) the new creation; just as "flesh and blood cannot inherit the kingdom of God" (1 Corinthians 15.50), the resurrection body has no place in the present created order. Also, the idea that the dead are already experiencing the fullness of salvation isolates their salvation from the salvation of the living and from the salvation of the world. He writes:

> We must retain a recognition that the fullness of salvation is still to come for the dead as well as the living ... Each time we pray for the coming of the kingdom we are praying for the dead as well as the living to enter into the completion of God's purposes. (Cocksworth 1997:17-18, abridged)

Those who die in Christ will be raised into the glory of God's kingdom, but not until God has come to his creation to bring it to its glory – the new creation, the consummation of creation-in-the-beginning, the marriage of heaven and earth. (Revelation 21.2).

The resurrection of the dead and the life eternal

In First Corinthians, Paul writes, "If for this life only we have hoped in Christ, we are of all people most to be pitied" (1 Corinthians 15.19). When Paul wrote to the fledgling church that he had founded several years earlier in Corinth, a large and prosperous port city in southern Greece, he was writing only twenty years or so after Jesus' death, resurrection and ascension. It appears that, amongst other things, he wanted to clear up for the Corinthians some sort of a confusion that existed about the resurrection of the dead, and to answer the question: what do we hope for after death?

Paul is clear that resurrection is not merely restoration to the life we have now but a triumphant transformation of our mortal bodies into something new and eternal. It does not mean the return to earthly life; rather it involves a metamorphosis into the new life of a new body. It will not be the body we have now – which is what Judaism believed with its imagery of corpses rising from their tombs and walking about. No, flesh and blood cannot inherit the kingdom of God. Paul says we will be given a "heavenly body", "imperishable" and "immortal". Although he also calls it a "spiritual body" (1 Corinthians 15.44), he does not mean it is simply a spiritual survival after death – the survival of the human spirit only as a kind of disembodied soul. That is what the Greek philosophers believed, but resurrection is something else: it is the transformation of the whole bodily person to a life that surpasses mortal life. When Paul speaks of a spiritual body he means a living being never separated from the Spirit of God, the giver of life, so that it is a life that can no longer be ended by death.

But for this we must wait until Christ comes again. His coming again is promised throughout the New Testament, the

Greek word *parousia* (describing a ruler's state visit and meaning both "coming" and "presence") normally being used to convey this promise. Christ's work that was begun in his incarnation and earthly ministry – demonstrating the presence of the kingdom of God in both word and signs – will finally be completed at the consummation of the present age. These Christian beliefs about the "last things" (in Greek *eschata*), which include the second coming, the resurrection of the dead, the last judgement and the reign of God, are dealt with by a branch of theology we call "eschatology".

The coming of Jesus is the focus of Christian hope because his future is our future and that of all creation. The Christian story sees God as "the Alpha and the Omega" (Revelation 1.8, 21.6, 22.13), the first and the last, the beginning and the end of all created things, their source and their goal. It is a story that is not yet completed; the end of the story is still to come. In Jesus' future coming, God is coming to his creation to take it beyond all evil, pain and death into the glory of his own eternal presence. Jesus' story is unfinished until the story of the whole world is complete, and the world's story is unfinished until he comes to complete it. Only at the end of time, when history is completed, will the final meaning of all things – of human life itself – be understood. The coming of Jesus is not just the last event of world history but the event that ends history. It will be the revelation of all that is now hidden, the disclosure of the full and final truth of all who have lived and all that has ever happened, and at this moment the dead of all history will rise to life in the new creation.

In John 14, Jesus' promise is that his return to God will make it possible for us to join in the relationship that he and the Father share: "If I go and prepare a place for you, I will come again and will take you to myself, so that where I am, there you may be also." Jesus' promised return makes it known that nothing – not even death – can separate us from life with God; it will be the ultimate witness to the power of God over life and death, and it will mark the arrival of the new longed for age when we inhabit our own "dwelling place" in God's house that Jesus has prepared for us. This is the destination of our journey, and Jesus says, "You know the way to the place where I am going."

Thomas, however, perhaps like some of us, remains confused: "Lord, we do not know where you are going. How can we know the way?" But Jesus does not spell out for Thomas the destination of his journey, or try to describe for him the kingdom. Instead he replies that the way to the kingdom is *in him* and *through him*. He offers to become the way itself, as well as our constant companion as we journey along the way. He embodies the kingdom himself, so that we can see and experience – in him and through him – the very nature of the reign and realm of God. "I am the way," Jesus says, "and the truth, and the life. No one comes to the Father except through me." To know "the way" is thus synonymous with knowing Jesus himself, who makes the truth of God available to the world and is the way to life with God. In Jesus-the-way we encounter both the truth of God and life with God, just as Nicodemus did that dark night in Jerusalem.

Group Session

0.00   Bible Study

Read John 3.1-21, the whole of the dialogue between Jesus and Nicodemus. Why does verse 13 refer to Jesus' ascension (an event that has not yet occurred in the context of this story) in the past tense? What does this tell us about the gospels and the things they say about Jesus? Can you find the story about Moses and the serpent in the wilderness (v. 14) in the Old Testament? (If someone in the group has an annotated Bible or "Study Bible" you will be guided to this very quickly, which proves just how useful they are!) **10 minutes**

0.10   Film Clip 1
Tom meets Sarah, who calls him "Boomer" (a member of the post-WW2 baby boom generation) in a derogatory manner. **5 minutes**

0.15   Brainstorm
What did you find interesting or thought-provoking in that clip? What issues or questions does it raise for you? Was there anything you didn't understand and would like to have clarified? **5 minutes**

0.20   Group Discussion
What do we learn about Sarah from this clip and what do you think of her? How does Tom react to her and how might you have responded differently? What might her enemies be? **10 minutes**

0.30   In Small Groups
What do you think of Cocksworth's three interpretations of "resting in the peace of Christ"? How do you like to think of your departed loved ones in relation to this schema? Do you think there are any other possible interpretations? **10 minutes**

0.40   Feedback and Share
Leader: allow each small group to feedback and share with everyone else some of the things they have talked about. **5 minutes**

0.45   Film Clip 2
Here we meet Jack. **5 minutes**

0.50   Brainstorm
What did you find interesting or thought-provoking in that clip? What issues or questions does it raise for you? Was there

anything you didn't understand and would like to have clarified? **5 minutes**

0.55 Group Discussion

What do we learn about Jack from this clip and what do you think of him? What do you think is going to happen (or not happen) if Tom doesn't start opening up and letting people in? Do you believe in miracles? **10 minutes**

1.05 In Small Groups

If this was *The Wizard of Oz* and Tom is Dorothy following the Yellow Brick Road to the Emerald City, who is the Tin Man (no heart), the Scarecrow (no brain) and the Cowardly Lion (no courage)? Who is the Wizard of Oz? What other connections can you make between the two films? **10 minutes**

1.15 Feedback and Share

Leader: allow each small group to feedback and share with everyone else some of the things they have talked about. **5 minutes**

1.20 Meditation and Prayer

Reader 1

Then Jesus said to [Zacchaeus], "Today salvation has come to this house, because he too is a son of Abraham. For the Son of Man came to seek out and to save the lost." (Luke 19.9-10)

Pause

[Jesus taught his disciples, saying,] "Pray then in this way: Our Father in heaven, hallowed be your name. Your kingdom come. Your will be done, on earth as it is in heaven. Give us this day our daily bread. And forgive us our debts, as we also have forgiven our debtors. And do not bring us to the time of trial, but rescue us from the evil one." (Matthew 6.9-13)

Pause

Blessed be the God and Father of our Lord Jesus Christ! By his great mercy he has given us a new birth into a living hope through the resurrection of Jesus Christ from the dead, and into an inheritance that is imperishable, undefiled, and unfading, kept in heaven for you, who are being protected by the power of God through faith for a salvation ready to be revealed in the last time. (1 Peter 1.3-5)

One minute's silence for reflection

Reader 2

An extract from *The Peaceable Kingdom* by Stanley Hauerwas, Professor of Theological Ethics at Duke University, North Carolina:

> It has long been noted that in the Gospels we have texts that indicate variously that the kingdom is coming, that it is present, and that it is still to come ... by letting the issue be dominated by the question of "when?" we miss the more important question of the "what?"
>
> The kingdom is not simply some cipher that we can fill in with our ideas about what a good society ought to look like. Nor is it merely a way of reemphasizing the eternal sovereignty of God, though this is certainly part of what the proclamation of the kingdom entails. Rather the proclamation of the coming kingdom of God, its presence, and its future coming is a claim about *how* God rules and the establishment of that

rule through the life, death, and resurrection of Jesus. Thus the Gospels portray Jesus not only offering the possibility of achieving what were heretofore thought to be impossible ethical ideals. He actually proclaims and embodies a way of life that God has made possible here and now.

Jesus directs our attention to the kingdom, but the early followers rightly recognized that to see what that kingdom entailed they must attend to his life, death, and resurrection, for his life reveals to us how God would be sovereign. Therefore to learn to see the world eschatologically requires that we learn to see the life of Jesus as decisive for the world's status as part of God's kingdom. (Hauerwas 2003:82-83, abridged)

One minute's silence for reflection

Reader 3

An extract from *Fortress Introduction to the Gospels* by Mark Powell, Trinity Lutheran Seminary, Columbus, Ohio:

In all of the Gospels, salvation has both present and future dimensions, but in Luke a decided shift can be observed toward the former. Luke does affirm the Christian hope for eternal life in "the age to come" (18:30), but in general he lays more emphasis on life that is possible here and now. We see this in the several verses, all unique to this Gospel, that make use of the word *today*.

In Luke, salvation may mean different things to different people. To a blind man, it means reception of sight (18:42) and to a leper it means being made clean (17:19). To others it may mean the reception of such blessings as peace (2:14) or forgiveness (7:48) or the removal of various infirmities (6:10; 8:48). Salvation for Luke is essentially *liberation*. Jesus the

Savior claims that he has come "to proclaim release to the captives" and "to let the oppressed go free." In Luke's story, Jesus saves people by liberating them from whatever it is that prevents their lives from being as God wishes their lives to be. In this regard, Luke makes no distinction among what might be construed as physical, spiritual, or social aspects of salvation. Forgiving sins, healing disease, and feeding the hungry are all saving acts. In Luke's theology, God is concerned with all aspects of human life such that salvation may involve righting any part of life that is not as it should be. (Powell 1998:105-106)

One minute's silence for reflection

Reader 4

I remember in your presence all my loved ones,
my fellow-prisoners,
and all who in this house
perform their hard service;
Lord, have mercy.
Restore me to liberty,
and enable me so to live now
that I may answer before you and before men.
Lord, whatever this day may bring,
your name be praised.
Amen.

(Dietrich Bonhoeffer, "Prayers for Fellow-Prisoners, Christmas 1943", in *Letters and Papers from Prison*)

Week Three: Who Can be Saved?

A Samaritan woman came to draw water, and Jesus said to her, "Give me a drink." (His disciples had gone to the city to buy food.) The Samaritan woman said to him, "How is it that you, a Jew, ask a drink of me, a woman of Samaria?" (Jews do not share things in common with Samaritans.) Jesus answered her, "If you knew the gift of God, and who it is that is saying to you, 'Give me a drink,' you would have asked him, and he would have given you living water." (John 4.7-10, *Lent 3, Year A*)

Prelude

En route from Judea to Galilee, Jesus took the direct road through the territory of Samaria, arriving in a city called Sychar (now Nablus) near Jacob's well. The feud between Jews and Samaritans had been festering for centuries. Samaritans were the remnant of the northern kingdom of Israel; they had inter-married with their Assyrian conquerors and their Judaic faith had absorbed certain elements of pagan religion. To their Jewish neighbours they were unclean, and to share a cup with one of them was to contaminate yourself. They were outsiders and enemies and – more than that – this one was a woman! Jewish rabbis would not even greet a Jewish woman in public, not even their own wife or daughter. Worse still, this Samaritan woman, we discover, was a woman of dubious moral standards. That is why she always came to the well in the heat of the midday sun when everyone else was indoors, to make a little easier her daily walk of shame.

Being so distant in time and culture we struggle to grasp the radical nature of Jesus' encounter at Jacob's well. It really was a "triple whammy" in terms of people one just did not speak to, especially if you were a rabbi and a holy man like Jesus. No wonder the disciples, as we learn, were so shocked. But Jesus was not like other rabbis and holy men. Social rules didn't seem to bother him much and, thirsty and tired, he is prepared to let even the lowest of the low give him a drink. And throughout the gospels we find him treating barriers with indifference. He sees beyond stereotypes and prejudices right through to the person, created in the divine image, fallen maybe, but still dearly loved by God. The long-excluded and looked-down-upon had been drawn into the circle of God's grace.

That is the power of the "living water" that Jesus offers – the life-giving water, the water of life. The late Malcolm Muggeridge once preached a sermon in Queen's Cross Church, Aberdeen, in which he reflected on his life in journalism and television, a life of considerable fame and material success. He said:

> Yet I say to you, and I beg of you to believe me, multiply these tiny triumphs by a million, add them all together, and they are nothing – less than nothing, a positive impediment – measured against one draught of that living water Christ offers to the spiritually thirsty, irrespective of who or what they are. (www.worldinvisible.com)

This week we need to consider the question "who can be saved?" This is not about whether "bad" people can be saved or not – we will deal with that next week when we explore the question "what do we have to do to be saved?" This week is about whether only *Christians* can be saved. What about people of other faiths or none? Is salvation only available to those who believe in Jesus, who said, "No one comes to the Father except through me" (John 14.6)? Is Jesus Christ the only way to salvation?

Through frequent reference and allusion to the exodus we have already established that Judaism is intrinsically linked to a belief in God's saving power, the exodus event itself being used as a model for future salvific events and as a basis for subsequent theological reflection. Islam, too, the third great monotheistic religion alongside Judaism and Christianity, is also a religion of salvation. These three "Abrahamic" faiths together share a belief in the same one true God, whom they call by different names. Muslims believe in the forgiveness of sins, salvation and a bodily resurrection on the Day of Judgement to everlasting life in the world to come. Life after death (*Ākhirah*) in Paradise (*Jannah*) is the ultimate goal of humankind:

> There is a reward in this present world for those who do good, but their home in the Hereafter is far better: the home of the righteous is excellent. They will enter perpetual Gardens graced with flowing streams. There they will have everything they wish. (The Qur'an 16.30-31)

Salvation is not, therefore, a specifically Christian idea, and Christianity is not in any sense distinctive or unique in attaching importance to the notion of salvation. As a result, it would be a good thing if we were able to give a proper account of what Christian theology has to say when it comes to the salvation of non-Christians. But be warned! This is a complex area. It is, nevertheless, one of the most important issues facing Christians in our modern world of religious diversity.

Three approaches

When speaking about salvation, Christian theology has three broad approaches to understanding the relationship between Christianity and other religious traditions. These are called exclusivism, inclusivism and pluralism.

> 1) *Exclusivism* (sometimes called "particularism") holds that only those who hear and respond to the Christian gospel may be saved. It is a conviction frequently encountered in the New Testament, for example in Paul's words, "For I am not ashamed of the gospel; it is the power of God for salvation to everyone who has faith" (Romans 1.16). Critics of this

approach often object to it on the grounds that those who, through no fault of their own, have not heard the good news of God in Christ are consequently denied salvation. This would be inconsistent with the Christian belief in the universal saving will of God, "who desires everyone to be saved and to come to the knowledge of the truth" (1 Timothy 2.4).

In fact Paul himself raises the question: "How are [people] to believe in one of whom they have never heard? And how are they to hear without someone to proclaim him?" (Romans 10.14). Karl Barth (1886-1968) argued that *at the end of time* God's grace will triumph over unbelief and all will come to faith in Christ. The difficulty with this hypothesis, however, is that it seems to regard salvation only as an eschatological event rather than as something that has meaning also as a life-changing experience in the here-and-now.

Central to exclusivism has always been the place of the Christian Church. The Church proclaims the gospel, and those who respond to the gospel and come to faith in Christ are, *de facto*, members of the Church. There was a time when the Church regarded herself to be "the ark of salvation", the adage *extra ecclesiam nulla salus* ("outside the church no salvation") communicating a particular belief that the Church, rather than Christ, was the mediator of salvation. In more recent times, however, there has been a shift from a Church-centred to a Christ-centred understanding of salvation, which makes a clear-cut distinction between the role of Christ and that of his Church.

2) *Inclusivism* recognises that there is only one Saviour, Jesus Christ: "There is salvation in no one else, for there is no other name under heaven given among mortals by which we must be saved" (Acts 4.12). Yet inclusivism also recognises that Christ's saving influence is effective beyond the bounds of the

Christian Church. The Holy Spirit moves throughout the whole world, in all places, cultures and religious traditions (not just amongst Christian communities), witnessing to the truth of God. Even though the saving presence of Jesus Christ is concealed from members of other religious traditions, it is no less real. In other words, salvation through Christ is possible for adherents of other faiths even though Christ remains unknown to them. Karl Rahner (1904-84), one of the most influential of modern Roman Catholic theologians, was perhaps the most prominent advocate of this approach. There is, then, salvation without the gospel (or Church) but not without Christ, whose saving work goes on even though it is unrecognised by many.

3) *Pluralism* involves a further shift from a Christ-centred to a God-centred understanding of salvation. Pluralism holds that all faiths give at least partial access to God and are legitimate means of salvation; all religions lead to the same God and Christians have no special access to God. A Christian may say that she has encountered life in Jesus, but that is not to say that this is the obligatory way for *all* human beings in every circumstance of time and place. To say "I believe in Jesus" is to say "I am saved through him", but this does not necessarily mean that he is the saviour of all. Jesus is the way for Christians, but other ways make him unnecessary for others. Advocates of this approach have no intention of undermining the faith commitment of Christians – or any other faith come to that. They argue only that Christianity must renounce its absolutist claims and recognise that other faiths provide for their adherents an equally legitimate path to salvation.

Such a viewpoint sits comfortably in the postmodern era, in which absolute or universal truth claims are rejected in favour of more relativistic views. These, by contrast, embrace the local and the diverse at the expense of the universal. We can never know for sure the way things are, only the way things are from within a particular standpoint. Accordingly, we must be careful not to confuse our own individual perspective with the abiding truth of reality itself.

The dignity of difference

It is not unreasonable to ask the question: why has God allowed so many religions to exist? Why has God made the search for truth so arduous amidst such a plethora of beliefs? Keith Ward identifies three main streams of religion: the Semitic stream, the Indian stream and the Eastern stream. He asserts, "There is no reason why a theist should not see God as at work to reveal and liberate in all three streams" (Ward 1998:154). Diverse cultures and histories are bound to produce different ways in which God's saving work is understood – something that is itself beyond adequate human comprehension. God has revealed his perfect truth in different ways, and these diverse religious traditions, which have come to know God in different ways, each bear witness to a non-exclusive truth imperfectly understood.

Perhaps we could surmise for now that God has a plan for humankind in which all these religions have a role to play, and only beyond this earthly life – when we come face to face with the truth (1 Corinthians 13.12) – might we understand more fully the importance of so many different worldviews. In the meantime, we ought not to press upon others the particularity of our own truth claims, nor argue about which religion is superior to others; rather we should seek to grow together in our under-standing of the truth that God has revealed. Above all, we need to respect what the Jewish Rabbi, Jonathan Sacks, calls "the dignity of difference". Difference should not be grounds for suspicion or hostility but grounds for theological and spiritual dialogue and understanding. He suggests that in the very diversity of faiths and cultures we will, if we listen carefully, hear the voice of God telling us something we need to know: "We will make peace only when we learn that God loves difference and so, at last, must we" (Sacks 2003:23).

Once it was Jews who were despised and persecuted by Christians, with both the Church and the Bible facing charges of anti-Semitism through the ages. St John Chrysostom (347-407) described the synagogue as "a place of meetings for the assassins of Christ", and Martin Luther (1483-1546) called for synagogues and Jewish schools to be set on fire (*Against the Jews and Their Lies*, 1542). Nazi picture books for children carried the caption, *Der Vater der Juden ist der Teufel* ("The Father of the Jews is the Devil"), a paraphrase of John 8.44. Perhaps it is no wonder, then, that Eliezer Berkovits has written:

> Christianity's New Testament has been the most dangerous antisemitic tract in history. Its hatred-charged diatribes against the Pharisees and the Jews have poisoned the hearts and minds of millions and millions of Christians for almost two millennia. (Berkovits quoted in Lloyd Jones 2000:211)

Muslims, too, have been the victims of persecution and genocide perpetrated by Christians. During the 1992-95 war in Bosnia, an ethnic cleansing campaign was waged by Bosnian Serb forces against Bosnian Muslims and Croats. In Srebrenica alone, 8,000 Muslim men and boys were massacred in 1995, and more than 25,000 others expelled from their homes.

Today, Muslims are mostly feared and mistrusted by Christians. Since 9/11, and as a consequence of subsequent Islamist terrorist atrocities throughout the world, an unhealthy and often irrational dread of Islam has taken hold in Britain and the West. This "Islamophobia" has sharpened pre-existing prejudices against Islam and heightened the need for inter-faith dialogue between Christians and Muslims. An important part of this conversation is a theological and spiritual dialogue that seeks to focus on the things that Christianity and Islam share in common, rather than on the things that divide them and over which they choose to disagree. One of these, as we have seen, is the notion – if not the actual means – of salvation.

Defending our faith

Even if we accept what has been said above about there being different ways in which God's saving work can be understood, we might still wish to prevent Christianity being relegated to the status of just one more faith among others. So how can we defend Christianity against the relativistic pluralism of the postmodern world? How can we stand up for the central Christian conviction that Jesus Christ is the unique and decisive revelation of God for the salvation of the world, without undermining the beliefs of other religious faiths?

It is, of course, a fine balancing act. On the one hand, to uphold the one holy catholic and apostolic Church as the mediator of God's salvation (exclusivism) is to deny the hope of salvation to anyone outside the Church. On the other hand, to affirm the efficacy of other faiths as ways to salvation (pluralism) is to deny the uniqueness of Christ. However, affirming the uniqueness of Christ is not the same thing as saying that God rejects those of other faiths; their salvation, too, it may be argued, is accomplished through the person and work of Jesus (inclusivism). This means that we should look for – and expect to see – signs of God's grace in the lives of non-Christians. We should enter into a dialogue with people of other faiths about the meaning and goal of God's purposes in history. And finally, as part of that dialogue, we must tell our story: the story of God's saving work throughout human history centred on the person of Jesus. But we need to do this with great sensitivity and respect for others and not with the intention of converting them – that is in God's hands alone.

Inclusivism seems to offer the best approach to understanding the relationship between Christianity and other religious traditions on the matter of salvation. The Roman Catholic theologian, Gavin D'Costa, puts it like this:

> The form of inclusivism I have argued for tries to do full justice to [the] two most important Christian axioms: that salvation comes through God in Christ alone, and that God's salvific will is truly universal. (D'Costa quoted in Dupuis 2001:193)

Inclusivism alone succeeds in holding to the Christian belief that Jesus Christ is the necessary mediator of salvation (neglected by pluralism) whilst, at the same time, holding to the belief in the universal saving will of God (neglected by exclusivism). God's saving will is revealed uniquely through Christ yet is truly universal, just as the Samaritan woman discovered at Jacob's well that day in the heat of the midday sun.

Group Session

0.00   Bible Study

Read John 4.1-42, the whole of the story about Jesus and the woman of Samaria. What contrasts can be drawn between the Samaritan woman and Nicodemus, both in terms of who they are and how they respond to Jesus? What comparisons can be made between the Samaritan woman and John the Baptist? What is the "hour" that is "coming, and is now here" (v. 23), and how can it be both coming and already come? **10 minutes**

0.10   Film Clip 1

Sarah shares her deepest secrets with Tom. **5 minutes**

0.15   Brainstorm

What did you find interesting or thought-provoking in that clip? What issues or questions does it raise for you? Was there anything you didn't understand and would like to have clarified? **5 minutes**

0.20   Group Discussion
What are your views on the rights and wrongs of abortion? If you believe that Sarah has "sinned" by terminating her pregnancy, do you think that her present emotional pain has anything to do with her having sinned? What is the relationship (if any) between sin and suffering? **10 minutes**

0.30   In Small Groups
Which of the three approaches to understanding the relationship between Christianity and other religious traditions on the matter of salvation do you like best? If the salvation of people of non-Christian faiths can be accomplished through the person and work of Jesus, even though he remains unknown to them, can the same be said for people of no faith at all? If faith is a gift of God, why does it appear to be given to some and not to others? **10 minutes**

0.40   Feedback and Share
Leader: allow each small group to feedback and share with everyone else some of the things they have talked about. **5 minutes**

0.45   Film Clip 2
Tom's continued rejection of his well-meaning companions lands him in the police station. **5 minutes**

0.50   Brainstorm
What did you find interesting or thought-provoking in that clip? What issues or questions does it raise for you? Was there anything you didn't understand and would like to have clarified? **5 minutes**

0.55   Group Discussion

Do you agree with Tom that the others are "frauds" with only superficial reasons for walking the Camino? What are their reasons? Is Tom's overt reason (to honour Daniel's desire to complete the journey) any better or worse than theirs? **10 minutes**

1.05   In Small Groups

What do you think makes a true pilgrim on the road that leads to life? Is it necessary to endure hardship or suffering along the way? Can we say of faith (as of many other things) that if it doesn't cost you something you are left to question its value? **10 minutes**

1.15   Feedback and Share

Leader: allow each small group to feedback and share with everyone else some of the things they have talked about. **5 minutes**

1.20   Meditation and Prayer

Reader 1

For we know only in part, and we prophesy only in part; but when the complete comes, the partial will come to an end. When I was a child, I spoke like a child, I thought like a child, I reasoned like a child; when I became an adult, I put an end to childish ways. For now we see in a mirror, dimly, but then we will see face to face. Now I know only in part; then I will know fully, even as I have been fully known. (1 Corinthians 13.9-12)

Pause

On that day [the "day of the LORD"] living waters shall flow out from Jerusalem, half of them to the eastern sea and half of them to the western sea; it shall continue in summer as in winter. And the LORD will become king over all the earth; on that day the LORD will be one and his name one. (Zechariah 14.8-9)

Pause

Then the angel showed me the river of the water of life, bright as crystal, flowing from the throne of God and of the Lamb through the middle of the street of the city. On either side of the river is the tree of life with its twelve kinds of fruit, producing its fruit each month; and the leaves of the tree are for the healing of the nations. (Revelation 22.1-2)

One minute's silence for reflection

Reader 2

An extract from *The Gospel in a Pluralist Society* by Lesslie Newbigin, British missionary in India and one of the first Bishops of the Church of South India:

I believe that we must begin with the great reality made known to us in Jesus Christ, that God – the creator and sustainer of all that exists – is in his own triune being an ocean of infinite love overflowing to all his works in all creation and to all human beings. I believe that when we see Jesus eagerly welcoming the signs of faith among men and women outside the house of Israel; when we see him lovingly welcoming those whom others cast out; when we see him on the cross with arms outstretched to embrace the whole world and when we hear his whispered words, 'Father, forgive them; they know not what they do'; we are seeing the most funda-mental of all realities, namely a grace and mercy and loving-kindness which reaches out to every creature. I believe that no person, of whatever kind or creed, is without some witness of God's grace in heart and conscience and reason, and none in whom that grace does not evoke some response – however feeble, fitful, and flawed. (Newbigin in Gunton et al 2001:433-434)

One minute's silence for reflection

Reader 3

An extract from *The Apostles' Creed* by Wolfhart Pannenberg, Professor of Systematic Theology in the University of Munich, Germany:

It has often been asked: if God was revealed in Jesus for the first time, and if salvation for mankind only appeared in Jesus, what is to happen to the multitude who lived before Jesus' ministry? And what will become of the many who never came into contact with the Christian message? What, finally, is to happen to the people who have certainly heard the message of Christ but who – perhaps through the fault of those very Christians who have been charged with its proclamation – have never come face to face with its truths? Are all these people delivered over to damnation? Do they remain shut out for ever from the presence of God which has been made accessible to mankind through Jesus?

The Christian faith can say 'no' to this urgent question ... what took place for mankind in Jesus also applies to the people who either never came into contact with Jesus and the message about him, or who have never really caught sight of the truth of his person and his story. In a way that is hidden from us – and in a way hidden even from themselves – the lives of these people may yet be related to the revelation of

God which appeared in Jesus ... So even the people who never knew Jesus are, in a way which neither they nor we can understand, also related to Jesus and the God whom he preached through the great context of humanity and its history. (Pannenberg 1972:94-95, abridged)

One minute's silence for reflection

Reader 4

Lord Jesus Christ,
you were poor and in distress,
a captive and forsaken as I am.
You know all man's troubles;
you abide with me
when all men fail me;
you remember and seek me;
it is your will that I should know you
and turn to you.
Lord, I hear your call and follow;
help me.
Amen.

(Dietrich Bonhoeffer, "Prayers for Fellow-Prisoners, Christmas 1943", in *Letters and Papers from Prison*)

Week Four: What Do We Have to Do to be Saved?

So for the second time [the Pharisees] called the man who had been blind, and they said to him, "Give glory to God! We know that this man [Jesus] is a sinner." He answered, "I do not know whether he is a sinner. One thing I do know, that though I was blind, now I see ... Never since the world began has it been heard that anyone opened the eyes of a person born blind. If this man were not from God, he could do nothing." (John 9.24-25, 32-33, *Lent 4, Year A*)

Prelude

Back once more in Jerusalem, Jesus encounters a man blind from birth. He spits on the ground and makes mud with the saliva, spreads the mud on the man's eyes, then sends him away to wash in the pool of Siloam (which John tells us means "Sent"). The pool of Siloam can still be seen today. It is fed by the Gihon Spring in the Kidron Valley, the water being diverted towards the city and channelled through a five hundred metre-long tunnel ending at the pool. Once it was an essential water supply when Jerusalem was under siege, but in Jesus' time it was used primarily for washing and bathing, perhaps of the ritual kind that was the precursor of Christian baptism. The healing of the blind man appears as a baptismal symbol in second-century frescoes in the catacombs in Rome, as does the story of the Samaritan woman at the well.

At the festival of Booths (or Tabernacles), the Jewish harvest festival commemorating God's protection of Israel during the wilderness journey after the exodus, the priests processed from the Temple to the pool of Siloam to draw water, returning through the Water Gate. This "water of salvation" was then poured on the altar as a libation. John's note about the pool's name meaning "Sent" implies that Jesus, sent by God, was present in the water with his power to save.

When the blind man returns from the pool he is able to see. Spittle and mud may simply have been a kind of natural medicine commonly used by healers at the time, but for John it was clearly significant because he details the use of spittle, mud and washing not only once but twice in his telling of this miracle story (cf. Mark 8.22-26). Whether this healing was natural or miraculous is not really important; what is important is that the blind man's sight was restored and he had to do nothing himself in order to receive this precious gift from Jesus. He didn't have to pray in the Temple every day, recite the Psalms, or even repent of his sins. In fact, he didn't even ask to be healed at all!

The story could be understood simply as a metaphor for the healing of *spiritual* blindness – "the light of the world" (v. 5) penetrating the "night" (v. 4). But even if that is so, the man's illumination remains a gift from God for which nothing had to be given in advance or offered in return. In reality, it seems that he gained both physical sight and spiritual insight at the same time, because after the healing he recognises Jesus as being "from God" (v. 33). He sees and believes. Recognising that Jesus' saving power flows directly from God, he is brought to the point of declaring his faith (v.38). The physical healing becomes an outward sign of his spiritual healing; faith and new life go hand-in-hand.

Amazing grace

In 1743, John Newton (1725-1807) was press-ganged into service as a midshipman in the Royal Navy and, in 1745, became embroiled in the Atlantic slave trade aboard the slave ship *Pegasus*. Three years later he experienced the beginnings of his conversion to Christianity when his ship encountered a severe storm off the coast of Donegal and was holed. As the ship filled with water, Newton called out to God to save him, at which moment the cargo shifted in the hold and stopped up the hole. The ship was able to drift to safety for repair. The following year, as first mate aboard the slave ship *Brownlow*, Newton became sick with fever in West Africa and asked God to take control of his destiny. He acknowledged the inadequacy of his spiritual life and professed his full belief in Jesus Christ. Nevertheless, he did not renounce the slave trade, and from 1750-54 he was captain of the slave ships *Duke of Argyle* and *African*. He gave up seafaring in 1754 after suffering a severe stroke and, in 1757, applied for ordination in the Church of England.

As an Anglican priest, Newton became a friend and ally of William Wilberforce, leader of the Parliamentary campaign to abolish the slave trade, and later apologised for his part as "an active instrument in a business at which my heart now shudders." In his great hymn, *Amazing Grace*, he reflected on his salvation:

Amazing grace! How sweet the sound
that saved a wretch like me.
I once was lost, but now I'm found;
was blind, but now I see.

Like the man blind from birth, whose words were clearly on his mind, Newton recognised God's saving power at work in his life. A wretch, lost and blind, had been saved by the transforming power of God's grace – the unconstrained and undeserved divine favour and loving mercy of God – not by any act of merit or deserving on his part. God, by grace, accepts us just as we are, and no one is beyond the compass of God's grace.

As we saw in Chapter Two, the pre-Reformation Western Church had come to the point of subverting the doctrine of grace through its obsession with "works" – acts of penance for the remission of sins and acts of merit (spiritual credit) or benevolence – all intended to help the living and their departed loved ones secure their place in heaven. Christians were made to live in perpetual fear of eternal damnation unless they took some action to save their souls. This, as we saw, was one of the reasons why pilgrimage grew in popularity. The idea of forgiveness by grace had become corrupted into the purchase of God's favour. Martin Luther (1483-1546), turning to the New Testament and especially the Letters of Paul, reasserted that salvation is God's free and gracious gift given to humanity in the atoning work of Christ; it is not something that can be bought or earned. As Carter Lindberg explains:

> Luther's biblical study led him to the conviction that the crisis of human life is not overcome by striving to achieve security by what we do, but by the certainty of God's acceptance of us in spite of what we do ... Luther now never tired of proclaiming that the burden of proof for salvation rests not upon a person's deeds but upon God's action. (Lindberg 1996:67, abridged)

Salvation is not about what we need to do to achieve it but what God has already done for us in Christ. A helpful acronym is: **G**od's **R**iches **A**t **C**hrist's **E**xpense. We are saved only by God's grace, not by any act of merit or deserving on our part, and *sola gratia* ("grace alone") became one of the great cries of the Reformation.

By grace alone through faith alone

The other slogan that resounded throughout much of sixteenth-century Western Europe was *sola fide*, "faith alone". God's grace most certainly prevails over a person's deeds, but certain passages in the New Testament make it clear that for salvation to be operative it is necessary to have faith. Jesus commonly says, "Your faith has saved you" (e.g. Luke 7.50), or "Your faith has made you well" (e.g. Mark 5.34). Paul writes:

> The righteousness of God has been disclosed ... through faith

in Jesus Christ for all who believe. For there is no distinction, since all have sinned and fall short of the glory of God; they are now justified by his grace as a gift, through the redemption that is in Christ Jesus, whom God put forward as a sacrifice of atonement by his blood, effective through faith. (Romans 3.21-25, abridged)

Remember here that Paul is writing to Christians in Rome, and we must be careful not to contradict what was said last week about those who have either not come into contact with the gospel or never really caught sight of its truth. But these are some of the most important words of Paul's teaching on "justification by faith", which is a key theme in Romans, his longest and possibly last letter and certainly his *magnum opus*. Justification by faith means that the sinner – and all of us are indicted – is "justified" (meaning declared righteous by God) because of the "righteousness" of God himself, which Paul understands to mean that which puts right the broken relationship between God and sinful humanity. The words "through faith in Jesus Christ" (v. 22) do not actually refer to *our* faith but may be better translated as "through the faithfulness of Jesus Christ". Therefore, in the cross of Jesus, the righteousness of God has been disclosed through *his* faithfulness for those who respond to it in faith.

Thankfully, Paul says the same thing in rather fewer words in Romans 1.17: "The righteousness of God is revealed through faith [God's faithfulness] for faith [the human response to it]." In other words, the righteousness of God is not a demand to be met by achievement but a gift to be accepted by faith. Justification is not what the sinner achieves but what the sinner receives.

This can lead to the misunderstanding that faith itself is an achievement – something that involves going to church every Sunday, something difficult and demanding that has to be worked at, a set of complex doctrines (like this one!) that need to be wrestled with and understood. But that is not so. Faith, in this context, is simply a relationship with God based on trust in the promise of God that "everyone who calls on the name of the Lord shall be saved" (Joel 2.32, Acts 2.21, Romans 10.13). Just as Newton aboard his sinking ship called out to God to save him, so a soldier under artillery bombardment on the battlefield will cry out, "Lord, save me!", as did the psalmist (Psalm 69.1) and Peter when he tried to walk on the water (Matthew 14.30). This is faith that suggests confidence in God's saving power; it is a faithful response to God's grace "however feeble, fitful, and flawed" (Lesslie Newbigin, Week Three).

If salvation is the free gift of a loving God, we become aware that this can only be so insofar as we make ourselves accessible to the saving power of God that Christ makes available to us. We have to put our life at God's disposal, holding ourselves open and ready before his forgiving grace and accepting his grace. We must surrender all our claims to self-importance, self-reliance and self-dependence. Salvation can only really be seen as God's gift if it is also the desire and the decision of the person to whom the gift is offered to receive it. Salvation is the divine initiative yet, in order for salvation to be God's real work in human life, it cannot be exclusively God's work – it becomes also a matter of our doing. We have the free will either to accept the gift or decline it; faith in Christ is our acceptance of that gift.

So, we are saved *by* grace *through* faith: "If you confess with your lips that Jesus is Lord and believe in your heart that God raised him from the dead, you will be saved" (Romans 10.9). We don't have to do anything else; we don't have to do anything good and it doesn't matter if we do anything bad.

But wait a minute! Not so, says James the Just, whose own epistle appears to contradict Paul's teaching on justification by faith: "What good is it, my brothers and sisters, if you say you have faith but do not have works? Can faith save you?" (James 2.14). He concludes it cannot: "Faith by itself, if it has no works, is dead" (James 2.17). Luther didn't like that because he held

Paul's teaching on justification by faith to be of central importance, and he questioned whether the Letter of James should ever
have found its way into the canon of scripture at all.

Paul seems to understand that good works are the natural
consequence of faith, because God is at work in us to give us both
the will and the ability to work for his good pleasure. To the
Ephesians he writes, "We are what [God] has made us, created in
Christ Jesus for good works, which God prepared beforehand to
be our way of life" (Ephesians 2.10). And to the Colossians he
writes that he and Timothy have not ceased praying for them,
"that you may lead lives worthy of the Lord, fully pleasing to
him, as you bear fruit in every good work" (Colossians 1.10).
These words suggest that Paul believes our good works to be a
gift of God in creation and the direct fruit of our regeneration by
the Holy Spirit. They are in no sense a human ground for self-
justification, which is why he tells the Philippians to "work out
your own salvation with fear and trembling" (Philippians 2.12).
The obedience shown by Jesus to his Father's will is now
expected of them; they are called to live each day in the reality of
what God has already done, to labour in obedience and reverent
fear (love) of God in response to God's gift of salvation, but their
works are God's works and will not be counted to their credit on
judgement day.

Judgement and hell

The New Testament speaks in many places about the Day of
Judgement, a great law court scene, future and final, that will
accompany the return of Christ. All will be judged, every aspect
of life will come into account, and Christ himself will be the
judge. Nowhere are these facts more clearly asserted than in the
parables of Jesus.

We will all be judged, the living and the dead, in respect of our
stewardship of the gifts, opportunities and responsibilities
granted to us during the course of our lives. What will be judged

is the appropriateness of a life for entry into God's eternal kingdom of justice and peace. As we have explored above, Paul believed that sinners (that is all of us) who trust in the perfect merit and finished work of Christ as Saviour have a guarantee of acquittal. They are "justified" – declared righteous by God at his judgement seat – not through any righteousness of their own but through God's. Christ's faithfulness, his perfect obedience in life and death, are imputed to them here and now and will stand to their account on judgement day. In Tom Wright's words, "The early Christians believed that *the verdict had already been announced* in the death and resurrection of Jesus" (Wright 1993:458).

The future existence of those who are not acquitted is referred to in the New Testament as "hell". Hell is the English rendering of the Greek word *Gehenna,* in turn derived from the Hebrew for "the valley of Hinnom", a place near Jerusalem where children were sacrificed by fire in pagan rites. In later Jewish writings, hell came to mean the place of punishment for sinners and was depicted as a place of unquenchable fire. The New Testament writers endorsed this past belief (e.g. Mark 9.43), and described it also as "darkness" (Matthew 25.30), "second death" (Revelation 2.11) and "separation from the presence of the Lord" (2 Thessalonians 1.9).

I cannot conceive of hell as a place where the devil stokes the fires of eternal torture and punishment, any more than I can conceive of heaven as a place where angels sit on clouds around God's throne playing harps. But I can form a conception of hell in terms of "separation from God". If, as we established in Week One, salvation means liberation from all that separates us from God, then hell aptly describes the state of being unsaved, of remaining in bondage to sin, evil and death. "My life is hell at the moment" is a statement that accurately defines an existence dominated by pain and suffering and experienced as apparent exclusion from the presence of the living God.

I believe that on the Day of Judgement God's verdict for everyone will be one of infinite mercy and forgiveness. No one will go unsaved. If Christian sinners are saved by grace through faith then I want to believe that non-Christian sinners can be saved too, even if in ways that are beyond our comprehension. All of God's creation can hope for the salvation that appeared in Jesus, because the Father did not send his Son to save just a few but to be "the Saviour of the world" (1 John 4.14). In John Macquarrie's words, "We must believe that God will never cease from his quest for universal reconciliation, and we can firmly hope for his victory in this quest" (Macquarrie 1977:367). The Apostles' Creed affirms that Jesus, after he had died and was buried, "descended into hell" (or "descended to the dead"). This was to proclaim the gospel "even to the dead, so that, though they had been judged in the flesh as everyone is judged, they might live in the spirit as God does" (1 Peter 4.6). In one of her visions, the fourteenth-century mystic Julian of Norwich went down to hell and found no one there.

What stands between the Jewish idea of hell and the last judgement is a dark, ugly, heavy instrument of Roman torture. It is also the instrument of God's unfathomable mercy and boundless love extended to all people who, like me, Newton, and the man blind from birth, have done nothing at all to deserve it.

Group Session

0.00   Bible Study

Read John 9.1-41, the whole of the story about Jesus and the man born blind. What do verses 3-5 tell us about Jesus' understanding of the relationship between sin and suffering, as distinct from that of the disciples (v. 2) and the Pharisees (v. 34)? Why do the Pharisees call Jesus a sinner (v. 24) and what does this tell us about their relationship with God? How is sin redefined by Jesus in this passage in such a way as to bring judgement on the

Pharisees themselves as sinners? **10 minutes**

0.10   Film Clip 1
A song called *Thank U* by Alanis Morissette accompanies the pilgrims as they continue on the long road to heaven. **5 minutes**

0.15   Brainstorm
What did you find interesting or thought-provoking in that clip? What issues or questions does it raise for you? Was there anything you didn't understand and would like to have clarified? **5 minutes**

0.20   Group Discussion
What signs can you see of God's grace at work in the lives of Tom, Joost, Sarah and Jack? What has happened to allow them to receive these riches? What is their response to God's grace? **10 minutes**

0.30   In Small Groups
One of the things that the song gives thanks for is "providence". What do you understand providence to mean? How does this differ from fate? What problems can result from a belief that God has a plan worked out for us in detail since time immemorial? **10 minutes**

0.40   Feedback and Share
Leader: allow each small group to feedback and share with everyone else some of the things they have talked about. **5 minutes**

0.45   Film Clip 2
The pilgrims reach the Iron Cross. **5 minutes**

0.50   Brainstorm

What did you find interesting or thought-provoking in that clip? What issues or questions does it raise for you? Was there anything you didn't understand and would like to have clarified? **5 minutes**

0.55   Group Discussion

Can you complete Sarah's unspoken prayer? What are the others laying down other than "a symbol of their efforts on the pilgrimage"? Can Tom's stone really weigh the balance in favour of his good deeds on judgement day? **10 minutes**

1.05   In Small Groups

Why does Jack think of churches as "temples of tears"? Have you ever thought of your own local church in this way? How does the universal Church bear witness to the bleeding, broken but deathless body of Christ? **10 minutes**

1.15   Feedback and Share

Leader: allow each small group to feedback and share with everyone else some of the things they have talked about. **5 minutes**

1.20   Meditation and Prayer

Reader 1

But God, who is rich in mercy, out of the great love with which he loved us even when we were dead through our trespasses, made us alive together with Christ – by grace you have been saved – and raised us up with him and seated us with him in the heavenly places in Christ Jesus, so that in the ages to come he might show the immeasurable riches of his grace in kindness toward us in Christ Jesus. For by grace you have been saved through faith, and this is not your own doing; it is the gift of God – not the result of works, so that no one may boast. (Ephesians 2.4-9)

Pause

She had heard about Jesus, and came up behind him in the crowd and touched his cloak, for she said, "If I but touch his clothes, I will be made well." Immediately her haemorrhage stopped; and she felt in her body that she was healed of her disease ... [Jesus] said to her, "Daughter, your faith has made you well; go in peace, and be healed of your disease." (Mark 5.27-29, 34)

Pause

As Jesus went on from there, two blind men followed him, crying loudly, "Have mercy on us, Son of David!" When he entered the house, the blind men came to him; and Jesus said to them, "Do you believe that I am able to do this?" They said to him, "Yes, Lord." Then he touched their eyes and said, "According to your faith let it be done to you." And their eyes were opened. (Matthew 9.27-30)

One minute's silence for reflection

Reader 2

An extract from *Christology Revisited* by John Macquarrie, Professor of Divinity Emeritus in the University of Oxford:

Simply because he is a person, Jesus Christ has to be known in ways that go beyond the historical data. In fact, there is a word for the special kind of relationship that the Christian has with Christ, the relationship in which he knows Christ, and that word is 'faith'. Faith is drained of its vitality if it is interpreted merely as belief. Certainly, faith will always contain belief, such as the belief ... that Jesus did really exist as a person in human history, and that the reports of his career in the New Testament are broadly reliable. But faith contains much more than belief, and is a more complicated relationship, with many strands to it. Faith has a different object from belief. We believe propositions, but we have faith in persons. Perhaps the best word to describe such faith is 'commitment', and this is an existential attitude of the whole man or woman. It was through faith in Christ that the first disciples began to perceive the 'more' in him and their understanding of him gradually deepened. There is reciprocity in the relation, as in all interpersonal relations. As the faithful disciple enters into a deeper understanding of Christ, so Christ imparts his own qualities to the disciples, and the latter's life too is deepened. (Macquarrie 2003:91-92, abridged)

One minute's silence for reflection

Reader 3

An extract from *Hope against Hope* by Richard Bauckham, Professor of New Testament Studies at the University of St Andrews, and Trevor Hart, Professor of Divinity at the University of St Andrews:

The crucified Christ bears already and representatively the full weight of God's final condemnation of sinners, but bears it in order that God's love might reach those under condemnation, bringing forgiveness and renewal of life. Those who by faith find in Christ their representative discover already, provisionally, God's verdict in their favour. The astonishing coincidence of God's utter condemnation of sinners and his radical grace for sinners occurs definitively in the cross and will recur at the last judgement. The last judgement will implement only what has been decided once and for all at the cross. From this perspective we can see that it is mistaken to think that God's judgement and God's mercy detract from each other, as though the more weight we give to judgement, the less we can give to mercy, and vice versa. Rather, there is direct proportionality between the two. God's mercy is as extensive as the severity of his judgement, and his judgement as uncompromising as the depth of his mercy ...

The Christ who is coming in judgement himself bore the judgement in love for us on the cross. To live in the light of final judgement means to remember that our lives are lived under God's scrutiny, to realize that we shall never cease to need God's mercy in Christ. (Bauckham and Hart 1999:143-145, abridged)

One minute's silence for reflection

Reader 4

O heavenly Father,
I praise and thank you
for rest in the night;
I praise and thank you
for this new day;
I praise and thank you
for all your goodness and faithfulness
throughout my life.
Amen.

(Dietrich Bonhoeffer, "Prayers for Fellow-Prisoners, Christmas 1943", in *Letters and Papers from Prison*)

Week Five: How are We Saved?

Martha said to Jesus, "Lord, if you had been here, my brother [Lazarus] would not have died. But even now I know that God will give you whatever you ask of him." Jesus said to her, "Your brother will rise again." Martha said to him, "I know that he will rise again in the resurrection on the last day." Jesus said to her, "I am the resurrection and the life. Those who believe in me, even though they die, will live, and everyone who lives and believes in me will never die. Do you believe this?" She said to him, "Yes, Lord, I believe that you are the Messiah, the Son of God, the one coming into the world." (John 11.21-27, *Lent 5, Year A*)

Prelude

A long, dark shadow lies over the small house in Bethany where Jesus had so often enjoyed the friendship and hospitality of his friends, Martha, Mary and Lazarus. In her anger and disappointment in Jesus, Martha is reproachful yet, at the same time, affirming of her faith in Jesus as a healer of the sick: "Lord, if you had been here, my brother would not have died." You might know what it's like to be in that place and to have the same "if only" thoughts. When we see death carry away someone who we love it is easy for us to blame God too. The shadow is dark indeed, life hurts, and we can't quite believe it will ever get better.

But a deeper healing than Martha had in mind is on offer: "Your brother will rise again." Martha interprets this as a statement of the widespread Jewish belief in a future resurrection of the dead on the "day of the LORD" (e.g. Daniel 12.2). But Jesus corrects her: the promise of resurrection and eternal life is not lodged in some distant event at the end of time, "on the last day", but is available already in the person of Jesus. Jesus identifies himself as the present fulfilment of future expectations, and asserts his rule and power over our present and future lives.

Physical death has no power over those who believe in his name. Martha's response, "I believe", is an affirmation of belief not in Jesus' statement or its logic but in the person of Jesus himself, and it is this belief that brings power in his name.

If you know how the story ends you will know that Jesus cries, "Lazarus, come out!" (v. 43), and Lazarus appears from the tomb in a miraculous way that prefigures Jesus' own resurrection from the dead. It was Jesus' showpiece miracle, his final sign before he himself becomes the sign, and whilst it concretely illustrates the truths about himself that Jesus has just declared it is these truths and not the miracle itself that have the lasting significance for the life of faith. Jesus' self-revelation as "the resurrection and the life" points to his sharing fully in God's power over life and death, and we see God's will for the salvation of the world at work in the world. It marks the beginning of God's new age, the age in which God's hope for the world becomes a reality. The power of death to remove people from life with God is reduced to nothing by the presence of the power of God in Jesus. The victory is won and the darkness that we fear is, in truth, the cradle of new life that we long for.

In this first week of Passiontide, the most solemn fortnight in the Christian year, it seems appropriate to explore the question: how does the cross "work"? The Christian Church has never laid down a single "doctrine of salvation"; rather there have emerged at various times in the Church's history a number of different "theories of the Atonement". Each sought to explain precisely *how* the mystery of the cross restores humanity to a right relationship with God, reconciling us to God, breaking down the walls of partition that separate us from God, so allowing us to enter into complete and inner communion with God and to be at one ("at-onement") with God. Each was couched in language and imagery that spoke clearly to the people of a particular time, and most theologians have drawn elements from one or more of the three main theories or "models" of the Atonement in their attempt to explain how the cross actually works.

The "Christus Victor" model (or "classic" theory)

The earliest model, Christus Victor ("Christ the Conqueror"), emerged with Christianity itself and was consolidated in the second and third centuries. It paints a picture of a cosmic battle between God and the devil. Known also as the "classic" theory, its central theme is a divine conflict and victory: Christ fights against and conquers the devil, a usurper who holds humanity in bondage to sin and death. In his authoritative work on the theories of the Atonement, first published in 1931, Gustaf Aulén writes:

> [The devil] is the lord of sin and death; he deceived mankind; and as men have followed him, they have fallen under his power, so that they may even be called his sons ... From the devil's dominion men cannot escape, except through the victory of Christ; and this victory is specially a triumph over the devil, for the devil is regarded as summing up in himself the power of evil, as he who leads men into sin and has the power of death. (Aulén 1965:26, abridged)

The defeat of sin and death puts the emphasis on salvation as the bestowal of life – fellowship with God and the partaking of the life of God. Salvation is new life; sin is a state of spiritual death and separation from God. As Paul says, "The wages of sin is death, but the free gift of God is eternal life in Christ Jesus our Lord" (Romans 6.23).

The Greek Church Father Irenaeus (130-202), in his concept of "recapitulation", stressed the many Pauline parallels between Adam and Christ: "the first man" vis-à-vis "the second man" (1 Corinthians 15.47); "the man of dust" vis-à-vis "the man of heaven" (1 Corinthians 15.48); "the one man's disobedience" vis-à-vis "the one man's obedience" (Romans 5.19). Here Christ recapitulates (or repeats) the history of Adam, succeeding at every point where Adam failed. The disobedience of Adam, which inaugurated the reign of sin and death, is annulled by the obedience of Christ who brings newness of life. Just as all humanity is present in Adam so too is it present in Christ, restored to perfection and righteousness before God: "For as all die in Adam, so all will be made alive in Christ" (1 Corinthians 15.22).

Origen of Alexandria (185-254) used the image of "ransom", drawing on the word used in Mark 10.45 – "to give his life a ransom for many." Origen suggested that God offered Christ to the devil as a ransom payment to secure the release of captive humanity, for humankind had become the devil's possession and was held under his power. The devil accepted the deal and gave up his prisoners, only to find that his possession of Christ was a torture he could not bear. Christ's goodness was too much for the devil and he was compelled to let him go. Humanity, which had been taken captive by the devil, was set free from the bondage of sin and death; the devil, who had taken humanity captive, was taken captive by God. This was the victory of the cross over the power of evil; good triumphed over evil, and this is why we call it *Good* Friday.

The "satisfaction" model (or "Latin" theory)

The language and imagery employed by the Church Fathers – the theologians whose writings helped to define the Christian faith in the first five centuries of the Church – was, by the Middle Ages, already losing its appeal. The classic theory was never wholly lost; indeed it resurfaced with greater power than ever before in Martin Luther and lives on today in liturgy, hymnody and art. However, in the medieval Western Church, Anselm of Canterbury (1033-1109) set aside both "recapitulation" and "ransom" in favour of a new theory of the Atonement, the "satisfaction" model, which he set out in his famous work *Cur Deus*

Homo? ("Why did God become Man?"). Here, in what is known also as the "Latin" theory, Christ's death provides the basis by which God is able to forgive sin rather than to conquer it. This is Aulén again:

> Its root idea is that man must make an offering or payment to satisfy God's justice; this is the idea that is used to explain the work of Christ. Two points immediately emerge: First, that the whole idea is essentially legalistic; and second, that, in speaking of Christ's work, the emphasis is all laid on that which is done by Christ *as man* in relation to God. (Aulén 1965:82-83)

It would be easy to make the connection in one's mind between the phrase "make an offering" and the Jewish practice of sacrifice. Indeed, Paul thought of Jesus as "a sacrifice of atonement by his blood" (Romans 3.25) and the Letter to the Hebrews contains much more on this theme. Gregory the Great (540-604) had pursued this motif, arguing that human sin necessitated a sacrifice. But no animal sacrifice could possibly be sufficient; a human being must be offered for the sin of humankind. The sacrifice must be pure and unblemished, but there is no person without sin (Romans 3.23). The only way forward was for the Son of God to become man, taking our human nature but not our sin (Hebrews 4.15, 1 John 3.5) and offering the perfect sacrifice of his precious body and blood.

However, in Anselm's mind it was not a sacrificial offering that had to be made to satisfy God's justice. In the medieval world of knights and chivalry, the idea of a "satisfaction" for sin would have been readily understood, perhaps as an opportunity to vindicate one's honour by fighting a duel, or as a just payment or other compensation owed for damage or injury. And, in the Latin Church, the word "satisfaction" would have been clearly recognised as something closely related to penance – the performance by a penitent after confession of an act prescribed by a priest for the remission of sins. For Anselm, the damage or injury was that caused by sin to *humanity* (not to God because he believed God to be impassible and so incapable of injury), and the satisfaction was Christ's death. Only a "God-man" would possess both the ability (as God) and the obligation (as a human being) to pay the required satisfaction. Through Christ's death God's justice is satisfied and the offence caused by human sin is purged.

The idea of satisfaction passes over easily into that of punishment. Anselm himself thought of Christ as enduring vicarious punishment, and Thomas Aquinas (1225-74), who built on many of Anselm's ideas, also spoke of Christ's work of satisfaction in terms of a punishment undergone on behalf of sinful humanity. Indeed, the concepts of satisfaction, penance and punishment are all closely related, and a later development of the satisfaction model, having its roots in the European Reformations, is known as the "penal substitution" model. This develops Anselm's satisfaction model from one where sin is purged *by the payment of a debt owed for injury* into one where it is purged *by the payment of a punishment for a crime*. God is just and his justice demands the punishment of sin; the only alternatives would be to condone sin or forgive it unjustly. But, rather than punishing humanity, God in Christ took upon himself the punishment for the sin of the world. Christ is understood here to be a substitute, the one who goes to the cross in our place. The punishment is paid by Christ as a man, living among men and women, and in their stead.

The "moral influence" model (or "subjective" theory)

Although it quickly gained widespread acceptance, the Latin theory soon found its first critic in Anselm's younger contemporary, Peter Abelard (1079-1142), who presented a very different understanding of the Atonement in the "moral influence" (or "example") model. Known also as the "subjective" theory, Abelard highlighted the *subjective* rather than the *objective* aspect of the cross. That is to say, rather than removing an objective barrier between humanity and God (i.e. sin) primarily what occurs is a change within human beings. Abelard saw Jesus' life and death as a demonstration of God's supreme and unfailing love, evident in Paul's words: "God proves his love for us in that while we still were sinners Christ died for us" (Romans 5.8). The subjective response of the sinner to this extraordinary act of love is to repent and turn to God, to love God in return and sin against him no more. The saved life is a life dynamically transformed from within, and one that recognises in this transforming experience the restoring work of God. Here is Aulén again:

> [Abelard] emphasizes especially that Christ is the great Teacher and Example, who arouses responsive love in men; this love is the basis on which reconciliation and forgiveness rest. Here he quotes Luke vii.47: "Much is forgiven to them that love much." This love awakened in men is treated by Abelard as meritorious; for even he cannot escape from the traditional Latin scheme of merit. (Aulén 1965:96)

Even though the response of love is deemed by Abelard – in accord with the mind of the period – to be "meritorious" (i.e. something done by a person that is seen as deserving of the reward of salvation), the real emphasis is on the merit of Christ. In his simple teaching grounded in the love of the Father, and through his death understood as a seal set upon his teaching and the supreme example of love (John 15.13), we find in his open arms the full expression of God's readiness to be reconciled to sinners. In response, we are drawn towards him in repentance and amendment of life; we receive his embrace and we are saved. Jesus' parable of the lost son and his loving father is the perfect illustration of this idea (Luke 15.11-32).

Abelard's theory exercised little influence in the Middle Ages,

being as it was far too radically opposed to the much loved satisfaction model to gain any real following. However, it enjoyed a
revival during the Pietistic movement of the seventeenth century,
which stressed the importance of personal feeling and
experience of God rather than the dogma of religion, and it
further consolidated its position in religious thought in the
eighteenth century during the intellectual movement of the
Enlightenment. The theologians of the Enlightenment challenged
all the bases of the Latin theory, which had come to be regarded
as the orthodox doctrine of the Atonement. In particular, they
argued that the legalistic and juridical notions of God that lay
behind the satisfaction model were relics of Judaism and were
inconsistent with the teaching of Jesus about the love of the
Father revealed in the New Testament. It was, therefore, a grave
error to imagine that God's justice needed to be assuaged
through a satisfaction offered to him, and that the death of Jesus
should be interpreted in this way. Instead, a more humanistic
and moralistic idea of the Atonement was propounded, which
involved a weakening of the notion of sin and a toning down of
the radical opposition of God to all that is evil.

Some people today would say that is a bad thing, though I am
not so sure. We began our study of salvation in Week One by
exploring baptism and the forgiveness of sins, and we have never
strayed far from the idea of sin since then. "Sin", "sinner" and
"sinful" are words that have occurred frequently in this book. So
the question I would like to end with is this: would God the Son
have become incarnate in Jesus of Nazareth, to die on a cross and
rise again, if humankind had never sinned? The Bible tells us he
would; it tells us that God intended the incarnation and self-
sacrifice of the Son *from eternity*. Matthew 25.34 speaks of "the
kingdom prepared for you from the foundation of the world",
and Revelation 13.8 of "the Lamb that was slaughtered from the
foundation of the world". The First Letter of Peter is equally
clear: "He [Christ] was destined before the foundation of the

world, but was revealed at the end of the ages for your sake" (1 Peter 1.20).

So why did Christ come? Sin and forgiveness are surely part of the answer, but the cross of Jesus was more than simply God's response to the predicament of sinful humanity; rather it was in some way part of the eternal purpose of God to perfect and complete creation. It was the ultimate self-revelation of a loving God to the world, and it would have happened even if the human race had remained free from sin. In Jesus' life and death we gain a glimpse of the character of the Most High God: "God is love" (1 John 4.8). Humanity is raised to a higher level – a more Christ-like state than before – because in Jesus we see the full possibilities of our human nature.

Jesus loved Lazarus and cried when he died (John 11.35-36). He raised him from the tomb in response to the love that he had for him – and for Mary and Martha. We must assume that Lazarus went on to die again, this time as the rest of us do, to rest in peace and rise in glory. Nothing – not even death itself – will be able to separate us from the love of God in Christ Jesus our Lord (Romans 8.38-39).

Group Session

0.00   Bible Study
Read John 11.1-44, the whole of the story about the death and raising of Lazarus. Why does Jesus, having received the message that Lazarus was ill, stay *two days* longer in the place where he was (v. 6)? What two things result from Jesus risking his life (vv. 7-8) to give life to his friend Lazarus? How do the final verses (43-44) differentiate the scene (and therefore this miracle) from the resurrection of Jesus? **10 minutes**

0.10   Film Clip 1
The pilgrims finally reach the heavenly city of Santiago de

Compostela. **5 minutes**

0.15   Brainstorm
What did you find interesting or thought-provoking in that clip? What issues or questions does it raise for you? Was there anything you didn't understand and would like to have clarified? **5 minutes**

0.20   Group Discussion
In what ways, metaphorically speaking, can we say that they have reached "heaven"? How have they each been changed? Are there any signs that they have come to faith in Christ? **10 minutes**

0.30   In Small Groups
Which of the three "theories of the Atonement" most appeals to you? Which do you think relates most closely to the experience of the characters we have followed in the film? Can we truly say that sin has been conquered? **10 minutes**

0.40   Feedback and Share
Leader: allow each small group to feedback and share with everyone else some of the things they have talked about. **5 minutes**

0.45   Film Clip 2
Having said that they wouldn't, the pilgrims continue to the coast. **5 minutes**

0.50   Brainstorm
What did you find interesting or thought-provoking in that clip? What issues or questions does it raise for you? Was there anything you didn't understand and would like to have clarified? **5 minutes**

0.55 Group Discussion

Where is Daniel now? How has Tom "made it" in more ways than one? Why does the ocean create a sense of awe and wonder and draw us deeper into the mystery of God? **10 minutes**

1.05 In Small Groups

What have you learned most from doing this course? Has your understanding of salvation substantially changed? Do you feel more confident now talking to others about the things you believe? **10 minutes**

1.15 Feedback and Share

Leader: allow each small group to feedback and share with everyone else some of the things they have talked about. **5 minutes**

1.20 Meditation and Prayer

Reader 1

In all these things we are more than conquerors through him who loved us. For I am convinced that neither death, nor life, nor angels, nor rulers, nor things present, nor things to come, nor powers, nor height, nor depth, nor anything else in all creation, will be able to separate us from the love of God in Christ Jesus our Lord. (Romans 8.37-39)

Pause

[Jesus said to his disciples,] "This is my commandment, that you love one another as I have loved you. No one has greater love than this, to lay down one's life for one's friends. You are my friends if you do what I command you. I do not call you servants any longer, because the servant does not know what the master is doing; but I have called you friends, because I have made known to you everything that I have heard from my Father. You did not choose me but I chose you." (John 15.12-16)

Pause

Beloved, let us love one another, because love is from God; everyone who loves is born of God and knows God. Whoever does not love does not know God, for God is love. God's love was revealed among us in this way: God sent his only Son into the world so that we might live through him. (1 John 4.7-9)

One minute's silence for reflection

Reader 2

An extract from *Exclusion and Embrace* by Miroslav Volf, Professor of Systematic Theology at Yale University Divinity School, Connecticut:

At the heart of the cross is Christ's stance of not letting the other remain an enemy and of creating space in himself for the offender to come in. Read as the culmination of the larger narrative of God's dealing with humanity, the cross says that despite its manifest enmity toward God humanity belongs to God; God will not be God without humanity. "While we were enemies, we were reconciled to God through the death of his son," writes the Apostle Paul (Romans 5:10). The cross is the giving up of God's self in order not to give up on humanity; it is the consequence of God's desire to break the power of human enmity without violence and receive human beings into divine communion. The goal of the cross is the dwelling of human beings "in the Spirit," "in Christ," and "in God." Forgiveness is therefore not the culmination of Christ's relation to the offending other; it is a passage leading to embrace. The arms of the crucified are open – a sign of a space in God's self and an invitation for the enemy to come in.

As an expression of the will to embrace the enemy the cross is no doubt a scandal in a world suffused with hostility. We instinctively reach for a shield and a sword, but the cross offers us outstretched arms and a naked body with a pierced side. (Volf 1996:126)

One minute's silence for reflection

Reader 3

An extract from *The Trinity and the Kingdom of God* by Jürgen Moltmann, Emeritus Professor of Systematic Theology at the University of Tübingen, Germany:

Even if we make the 'emergency' of human sin the starting point, so as to grasp the necessity of divine reconciliation, and in order to expect the coming of the divine Reconciler, we must go beyond the measure of human need if we are to understand grace as *God's* grace ...

According to Paul Christ was not merely 'delivered for our offences' but was also 'raised again for our justification' (Rom. 4.25 AV). Reconciling sinners with God through his cross, he brings about the new righteousness, the new life, the new creature through his resurrection. The justification of the sinner is more than merely the forgiveness of sins. It leads to new life: 'Where sin increased, grace abounded all the more' (Rom. 5.20). This is the way Paul expresses the imbalance between sin and grace, and the *added value* of grace. This surplus of grace over and above the forgiveness of sins and the reconciliation of sinners, represents the power of the new creation which consummates creation-in-the-beginning. It follows from this that the Son of God did not become man simply because of the sin of men and women, but rather for the sake of perfecting creation. (Moltmann 1981:115-116, abridged)

One minute's silence for reflection

Reader 4

In me there is darkness,
but with you there is light;
I am lonely, but you do not leave me;
I am feeble in heart, but with you there is help;
I am restless, but with you there is peace.
In me there is bitterness, but with you there is patience;
I do not understand your ways,
but you know the way for me.
Amen.

(Dietrich Bonhoeffer, "Prayers for Fellow-Prisoners, Christmas 1943", in *Letters and Papers from Prison*)

Chapter Four

El Camino

A Love Story

Leaving Burgos by the Malatos Bridge, Rachel passed the Hospital del Rey and followed the yellow way markers onto the path beside the Arlanzón River. It was half past eight in the morning and she had made an early start with the intention of reaching Hontanas by late afternoon. Hontanas, named after its springs of which there are few on the *meseta*, the arid plain of Old Castile, had a long tradition of hospitality and would be a good place to stop for the night.

She was walking on her own today as she always did, alone with her thoughts about where she had been and where she was going. She didn't really know where she was going, other than in the literal sense. She was headed west, of course, towards Santiago, but she didn't know where her life was going or whether she actually had a life at all. She had a life once, she was sure of that, but she didn't think that she had a life now. What the future held she had no idea, but it looked pretty bleak and she didn't think she would ever be happy again.

Before she met Peter she had probably never known true happiness in her life, being a bit of a loner through school and the sort of person who always found it difficult to make friends. She had certainly not been "in love" with anyone before Peter, and she didn't believe anyone had really loved her. She was an only child whose father had committed suicide when she was eight years old, something her mother never talked to her about – though Rachel wished that she had. Her mother went off the rails some years later, drowning her grief in alcohol and drugs, and Rachel was taken into care when she was fourteen. It was a deeply unhappy time, punctuated by bouts of bullying and sexual exploitation, and she was left feeling terribly alone. Until, that is, she met Peter. She was eighteen, he was twenty, and two years later they were married. They made a home together, planned to start a family together, and Rachel knew that they would grow old together. Peter was her rock and on that rock she built her life.

Peter died suddenly and unexpectedly whilst on their honeymoon in Greece, the result of multi-organ failure caused by acute food poisoning. The best two years of her life had come to an abrupt end. She was devastated by his death, his passing was unbearable, and she knew that nothing would ever be the same again. That was a year ago now, and Rachel was on the pilgrim road to Santiago in a vain attempt to make some sense of it all, to search for some meaning in Peter's death. She was wasting her time of course, she half-knew that already, because this heartbreaking tragedy was senseless and meaningless. Perhaps, in the end, she was simply hoping that a month on the *Camino* would allow enough time for some of her demons to walk away.

Reaching Hornillos at about one o'clock, a little over half way on her day's journey, Rachel paused to eat the sandwich she had bought on her way out of Burgos. Hornillos was quite unlike other Castilian villages, built in response to the pilgrimage and boasting a wide main street flanked on both sides by large mansions. As she sat on a bench in the shade beside the mud-baked road, her eye caught sight of a large cross inscribed on the lintel above the door of the house opposite. "What have you to do with me, Jesus, Son of the Most High God?" she thought to herself as she started hungrily on her *jamon y queso* sandwich. The thought didn't stay with her long. Rachel was not "religious" in any sense of the word. She was astonished that anyone could believe in God in the face of all the evil and suffering in the world. If there was a God, an all-loving and all-powerful God as people claimed he was, then why didn't he do something about it? If, in fact, he couldn't, then he seemed to her to be rather a pointless God and not worth believing in at all.

She reached into the side pocket of her rucksack and took out her e-reader. It came on at the page where she had last left it, part-way through Ernest Hemingway's *For Whom the Bell Tolls*, the novel inspired by his experiences as a war correspondent covering the Spanish Civil War. On the first leg of her journey, as she passed through Pamplona, she had read his other great Spanish novel, *Fiesta*, about the annual bullfighting festival where the bulls are run through the streets on their way to the ring. During her teenage years, Rachel had become an avid reader of Hemingway, trying to get inside the mind of a man who, like her father, had pressed the muzzles of a loaded shotgun to his forehead and fired both barrels. His novels were full of sadness and death, hammered out of the raw material of life – not least his own. He had once likened life to a game of baseball: they threw you in and told you the rules and the first time they caught you off base they killed you. They killed the very old and the very young, the good and the bad, the innocent without impunity. They always found a way to get you in the end. That was *her* religion Rachel thought: life is a struggle for survival in an unjust world of triumphant evil and endless suffering – and then you die.

She put the e-reader away, lifted on her rucksack, and started to walk. Once out of the town the pilgrim road, now a cart track, wound its way up again on to the crest of the high plain, starved of trees, starved of water, where the dry, impoverished soil was whipped into swirls of dust by the hot wind. As she passed through Sambol, close to the remains of the monastery of San Baudillo, a man came near and went with her. "*Ola!*" he said. "Do you mind if I walk with you for a while?"

Rachel was taken aback. She had walked alone every day out of choice and had many times given other well-meaning pilgrims the brush-off. But this man seemed different. He was English, about her age with kind eyes and a nice smile, and she was strangely drawn to him. "Okay," she replied hesitantly.

"My name's Josh," he said, "Josh Christie. I work at the Tourist Office in Santiago. It was a bit quiet this week so they let me walk the Way from Burgos to León to see if I could update their guidebook. It's just a summer job – I'm hoping to get a proper job as a Spanish-English translator one day!"

Rachel smiled and began, in a guarded way, to tell him a little about herself. But she soon found herself opening up to him completely, and before long she had told him everything about her father and about Peter. There was something about him that made her feel like she wanted to share it with him, to get it off her chest and cry on his shoulder.

As they walked and talked they came to a place where the path divided. To the left was a wide and easy track, and to the right a narrow, harder path, which wound its way up the hillside, overgrown and neglected, before quickly disappearing from sight amid the scrub and rock. Rachel automatically took the left fork, but Josh said, "No, let's go this way. Let's go through the narrow gate."

"But there is no gate," Rachel replied.

"I am the gate," Josh said, somewhat mysteriously, before bounding up the hillside through a thicket of brambles, leaving Rachel trailing in his wake. "Come on!" he shouted. "We can still get to Hontanas this way."

"Are you sure?" Rachel enquired nervously.

"Oh yes," said Josh, "I know the way."

Over the crest of the hill the path opened up and levelled out among eucalyptus trees and fertile meadows. It was an oasis of verdant beauty, watered by icy springs, where the hot afternoon sun was reduced to a cool, dappled light in the shade of the trees. As they followed an avenue of poplars, straight and level as far as the eye could see, Rachel knew there were few who found this way, yet it was the most beautiful part of her entire journey so far. To her left and right were endless fields of wheat and barley, still green and short in June, and when the tree-lined avenue eventually gave way to a path edged with yellow broom, red poppies and pink dog roses Rachel wished that this moment of her life would last forever.

As they came near Hontanas, hidden in the valley of a small river, Josh walked ahead as if he were going on. But she urged him to stay with her. "It's almost evening," she said, "won't you stay here the night as well?"

Josh agreed, and so they walked together down the steep path into the village and checked in to the *Albergue Santa Brígida*. It had two dormitories, each of seven beds, one for men and one for women, and cost six euros for the night. Pilar asked for their *credencials*, stamped them, and took their money. "Up the stairs," she said curtly, "men on the left, women on the right."

A couple of hours later, Rachel came downstairs and found Josh at a table outside drinking a *San Miguel*. "May I join you?" she asked tentatively.

"Of course," he replied, "and why don't we have supper together tonight as well?"

"That would be nice," she said. "Here?"

"No, it's another five euros and won't be all that great. There's a *casa rural* up the road with a good restaurant – why don't I treat you?"

"You're very kind," Rachel replied, "that would be lovely."

When Josh had finished his beer they walked to the restaurant, *El Descanso*, and were shown to a table by a waitress who was also called Pilar. "Why is everyone here called Pilar?" Rachel whispered to Josh.

"It's a popular girl's name in Spain," he replied. "It comes from the *Virgen del Pilar* or 'Virgin of the Pillar' in Zaragoza, where the Virgin Mary appeared to James in a vision. She was standing on the pillar to which Jesus had been tied for his flagellation."

"Do you believe in all that stuff?" she asked him.

"Well, some of it," he said. "James was certainly an apostle of Christ, but whether or not he really came to Spain I'm not so sure. But if he did, who's to say he never saw such an apparition?"

"But you believe in Jesus?"

"Oh yes, for sure – the resurrection and the life. Don't you?"

"No," Rachel replied, "I'm afraid I don't."

There was a silence. Josh made no immediate response and they both seized the moment to peruse their menus. After Pilar had taken their orders, the *paella* for Josh and the *tortilla* with *ensalada* for Rachel, Josh asked, "Why not? Why don't you believe?"

"I just can't see the evidence," Rachel said. "If God is good and righteous he's got a funny way of showing it. He's certainly done nothing for me. There's simply too much misery in the world."

"But that's exactly *why* Jesus came," Josh countered. "That's precisely the reason *why* God came into the world in human form: to show us what God is really like. And through his teaching about love and by laying down his life for others – the greatest act of love – help lift the world out of all evil and pain."

"Well, it doesn't seem to have had much effect yet."

"Maybe you're right," said Josh, "but we all have to do our bit to help – we have to respond in some way. God works through people."

This time Rachel was silent. She could think immediately of no adequate response, so she changed the subject altogether and asked him where he lived in England.

"In Oxbury," he replied.

"I know Oxbury!" she said. "It's just up the road from me in Winford."

"How extraordinary – what a small world! Well, I live in the block of flats opposite the Town Hall – between the cinema and a wine bar called *The Vine.*"

"I know where you mean," Rachel said, just as Pilar brought over a bottle of *riocha* with a large chunk of bread and a dish of olive oil and placed them down on the table. Josh poured them both a glass of the wine and said, "Would you like some bread?"

"Thank you, I would."

Josh broke the bread, gave it to her and said, *"Homonis vis."*

"Homo what?"

"Homonis vis – 'the strength of man'. It's Latin. It's how they came up with the name *Hovis.* Quite clever, don't you think? It's like 'the bread of life'."

After Pilar had arrived with their food and placed it down on the table, Josh asked Rachel, "Are you carrying a stone to place at the *Cruz de Ferro?*"

"The what?" she said, conscious that she was now starting to sound a bit dim.

"The Iron Cross. It stands on top of a huge cairn marking the highest point of the Way – 1,504 metres in the mountains of León."

"Oh yes, I've read about that, but I've not been carrying one. Should I be?"

"For medieval pilgrims it was a symbolic act, an act of contrition for sins. They carried their sins with them and laid them at the foot of the cross. But think of it more as representing the load you are carrying now – all your pain and your sorrow, the weight you want to cut loose and cast off. We'll pick up a stone for you tomorrow. 'Come to me, all you that are weary and are carrying heavy burdens, and I will give you rest'," he added, though Rachel didn't know exactly what he meant. But she found that she could talk effortlessly with this enigmatic stranger, and as he told her about his passion for the Way and everything that it meant to him there were moments when she felt her heart burn within her.

* * *

They walked together for the next seven days before reaching León, the city named after the Roman Seventh Legion that established its headquarters there in the year AD 68. As the week drew on, Rachel became increasingly sad at the thought of Josh having to leave and on the final morning, as they stood on the heights of the Alto del Portillo looking down on the city and the imposing towers of its cathedral, she could hardly bear that the end was in sight.

They descended the mountain to the Castro Bridge over the Torio River and entered the city via the Jewish quarter. Josh made straight for the railway station to catch a train to Santiago and Rachel went along too, not wishing to lose a single moment with him. As he boarded the carriage he said, "I've really enjoyed meeting you, Rachel. Take good care of yourself."

"I will," she said, with tears in her eyes.

The train pulled away. *Buen Camino!* he shouted from the window, and then he was gone.

Rachel felt empty and alone. She wandered around the city for a while and went into the great thirteenth-century cathedral, Spain's Gothic masterpiece, which has the finest stained glass in Europe. Despite its sublime luminosity, the light of the world creating a play of colours on the floor, she found that nothing could take her mind off Josh. She felt bereft by his absence and her only comfort was the knowledge that she would see him at the Tourist Office the moment she arrived in Santiago.

That evening in the *refugio*, as she unpacked her rucksack, she found a Bible. It wasn't hers and she presumed that Josh must have secreted it there sometime during the day. It was called the *Good News Bible*, which made her wonder whether there was a *Bad News Bible* as well. A page was marked and a passage highlighted – John chapter 10 verse 10: "I have come in order that you might have life – life in all its fullness." Rachel didn't really know what to make of it. She thought about it for a while as she got ready for bed and went to sleep with the Bible under her pillow.

* * *

The next two weeks without Josh passed painfully slowly. She walked alone every day and ate alone every evening, politely refusing the other pilgrims who invited her to join them, and when she reached the Iron Cross she laid down the stone that Josh had given her on the day they left Hontanas. As she placed the stone on the cairn at the foot of the cross, she said, "I love you, Pete, I always will. I'll never forget you, but I think it's time for me to try to move on now."

It was raining when she finally arrived in Santiago. She entered the city by the Puerta del Camino, as all pilgrims do, even though the gate and the walls it once penetrated exist no longer, and followed the last of the yellow way markers through the narrow streets to the cathedral. It was the end of her journey. In the square a piper was playing the bagpipes, a reminder of Galicia's Celtic history, and scores of pilgrims were milling about in groups, greeting and embracing each other, oblivious of the rain. Her first desire should have been to enter the cathedral and pay homage at the reliquary of the Apostle, but instead she hurried to the Tourist Office in the Rúa del Villar to see Josh.

The office was bustling with people. She went in, nervous and excited, and blurted out to the first official-looking person she saw, "Is Josh here? I've come to see Josh."

"I've no idea," the man replied. "There are many tourists here. Look for him yourself."

"No! He works here," Rachel said.

"There is no one working here called Josh."

"Yes there is! Josh Christie, an English guy."

"There is no one working here called Josh Christie," the

official said. "There are no English people working here at all. Now please move on."

Rachel was stunned. She stumbled out of the office in a daze and drifted aimlessly around the streets for a while before going to the Pilgrim Office to have her *credencial* stamped for the last time and collect her *Compostela*.

* * *

The next day at noon she went to the Pilgrims Mass in the cathedral. She couldn't remember the last time she had been to church, but this was one of the age-old rites of pilgrimage and supposedly the crowning moment of her endeavour. She didn't understand anything that was said because it was all in Spanish, but when the priest broke the bread and everyone started going up in line to receive she was strangely drawn and joined the long procession. She had never received communion before, but as she took the host into her mouth and swallowed it she felt a strange warmth flow through her. At the same time, though she couldn't quite explain it, she felt as if something else was leaving her, that something inside her was being purged. After she had sat down again in her seat, the organ of two thousand pipes began to play and the vast cathedral was filled with the most beautiful music she had ever heard. And then the *botafumeiro* began to swing, gently at first, but then higher and higher with each pendulum swing until it reached the highest point of the vault at each end of the transept. On every downward stroke it soared past her, just a few feet above her head, instinctively making her feel as though she ought to duck. And as the incense billowed out in great clouds and filled the cathedral with its perfume, and as the music from the organ reached a crescendo, she began to cry. She cried like she had never cried before. All the agony of her twenty-one years poured out of her; she cried for her father and for her mother, she cried for Peter, and she went on crying until the flagstone floor beneath her feet was flooded with her tears.

She left the cathedral and waited for a coach to the airport at A Coruña to catch the ten past six flight to Heathrow, arriving ten past seven local time. It was gone eleven o'clock when she arrived home in Winford and she collapsed exhausted into bed. She was still thinking about Josh, puzzled and disappointed that she had not seen him in Santiago, and she resolved that in the morning she would go to Oxbury to find out if he was already back home.

* * *

Rachel stood with her back to the Town Hall and looked across the street. There was only one building between the cinema and *The Vine* and it was a church, the Church of the Good Shepherd. She crossed the street and went inside, saddened and perplexed once more that her search for Josh had apparently reached another dead end. On the lectern there was a Bible, open at Deuteronomy chapter 30, and her eyes scanned the page: "Today I am giving you a choice between good and evil, between life and death ... between God's blessing and God's curse, and I call heaven and earth to witness the choice you make. Choose life."

She went back out on to the street and, seeing that the wine bar was open, decided that she needed a drink. She went inside and ordered a glass of wine. She took it to a table, sat down, and tried to make some sense of all that had happened over the past couple of days. Where on earth was Josh? *Who* on earth was Josh? Had she simply misunderstood everything that he had said to her about where he worked and where he lived?

After a few minutes, a man sitting alone at the next table reading a newspaper looked across to her and said, "Don't worry, it may never happen!"

Rachel looked at him. He looked a bit like Josh, but she knew immediately that it was not him. "Sorry," she said, "I've had a bad day."

"Can I join you?" he asked. "My name's Jake – Jacob really – but everyone calls me Jake."

"Um, no thanks," Rachel replied, "I was just leaving." She quickly drained her glass of wine and walked out of the bar. She started walking down the street towards the bus stop but suddenly stopped dead in her tracks. *Choose life*, Rachel remembered. *Choose life*.

She turned around and went back into the wine bar. She went straight up to Jake and said, "I've changed my mind. I'd love to talk to you if that's still okay with you."

"Of course it is," he said. "Let me get you another glass of wine."

* * *

Two years later, Rachel and Jake were married. They had a son, whom they named Benjamin, and they lived happily ever after. Rachel never forgot Peter and continued to visit his grave three times a year – on his birthday, on their wedding anniversary and at Christmas. She never forgot Josh either, because she knew in all truth that He was the One who had shown her the way that leads to life.

About the Author

The Reverend Tim Heaton is in parish ministry in the Diocese of Salisbury. He was ordained as a Deacon in 2008 and priest in 2010 at the age of 51. That same year, he was awarded a BA (Honours) Degree in Theology for Christian Ministry and Mission. Educated at Harrow and Sandhurst, he spent five years in the army before pursuing a career in the City of London. After twenty years he left the City in 2003 to answer his call to ordination. He lives in north Dorset with his wife Arabella.

E-mail: timheatonauthor@gmail.com

Facebook: www.facebook.com/lentcourses

Bibliography

All Bible quotations are from the *New Revised Standard Version* unless stated otherwise.

Abdel Haleem, M. A. S. (2005) *The Qur'an: A New Translation by M. A. S. Abdel Haleem*, Oxford: Oxford University Press.

Aulén, G. (1965) *Christus Victor: An Historical Study of the Three Main Types of the Idea of the Atonement*, London: SPCK.

Bauckham, R. and Hart, T. (1999) *Hope against Hope: Christian Eschatology in Contemporary Context*, London: Darton, Longman and Todd.

Bonhoeffer, D. (2001) *Letters and Papers from Prison: An Abridged Edition*, London: SCM Press.

Boring, M. E. (1995) "The Gospel of Matthew" in *The New Interpreter's Bible Volume VIII*, Nashville TN: Abingdon Press.

Cocksworth, C. (1997) *Prayer and the Departed*, Cambridge: Grove Books.

Culpepper, R. A. (1995) "The Gospel of Luke" in *The New Interpreter's Bible Volume IX*, Nashville TN: Abingdon Press.

Dupuis, J. (2001) *Toward a Christian Theology of Religious Pluralism*, Maryknoll NY: Orbis Books.

Gitlitz, D. M. and Davidson, L. K. (2000) *The Pilgrimage Road to Santiago: The Complete Cultural Handbook*, New York: St Martin's Griffin.

Green, J. B. and Baker, M. D. (2003) *Recovering the Scandal of the Cross: Atonement in New Testament and Contemporary Contexts*, Carlisle: Paternoster Press.

Gunton, C. E., Holmes, S. R. and Rae, M. A. eds (2001) *The Practice of Theology: A Reader*, London: SCM Press.

Hauerwas, S. (2003) *The Peaceable Kingdom: A Primer in Christian Ethics* (Second edition), London: SCM Press.

Lindberg, C. (1996) *The European Reformations*, Oxford: Blackwell.

Lloyd Jones, G. (2000) "Encountering the New Testament" in Rittner, C., Smith, S. D. and Steinfeldt, I. eds *The Holocaust and the Christian World*, New York: Continuum.

Macquarrie, J. (1977) *Principles of Christian Theology* (Revised edition), London: SCM Press.

Macquarrie, J. (2003) *Christology Revisited* (Second impression), London: SCM Press.

Moltmann, J. (1981) *The Trinity and the Kingdom of God: The Doctrine of God*, London: SCM Press.

Müller, P. and Fernández de Aránguiz, A. (2010) *Every Pilgrim's Guide to Walking to Santiago de Compostela*, Norwich: Canterbury Press.

Mullins, E. (2001) *The Pilgrimage to Santiago*, Oxford: Signal Books.

O'Day, G. R. (1995) "The Gospel of John" in *The New Interpreter's Bible Volume IX*, Nashville TN: Abingdon Press.

Pannenberg, W. (1972) *The Apostles' Creed in Light of Today's Questions*, London: SCM Press.

Perkins, P. (1995) "The Gospel of Mark" in *The New Interpreter's Bible Volume VIII*, Nashville TN: Abingdon Press.

Powell, M. A. (1998) *Fortress Introduction to the Gospels*, Minneapolis MN: Fortress Press.

Sacks, J. (2003) *The Dignity of Difference: How to Avoid the Clash of Civilizations* (Second edition), London: Continuum.

Studdert Kennedy, G. A. (2007) *Food for the Fed-Up*, Liskeard: Diggory Press.

The Archbishops' Council (2005) *Common Worship: Daily Prayer*, London: Church House Publishing.

Volf, M. (1996) *Exclusion and Embrace: A Theological Exploration of Identity, Otherness, and Reconciliation*, Nashville TN: Abingdon Press.

Ward, K. (1998) *God, Faith & the New Millennium: Christian Belief in an Age of Science*, Oxford: Oneworld.

Ware, K. (1995) *The Orthodox Way* (Revised edition), Crestwood

NY: St Vladimir's Seminary Press.

Wright, N. T. (1993) *The New Testament and the People of God: Christian Origins and the Question of God Volume One* (Second impression), London: SPCK.

Wright, N. T. (2006) *New Heavens, New Earth: The Biblical Picture of Christian Hope* (Second edition), Cambridge: Grove Books.

Circle Books

Circle is a symbol of infinity and unity. It's part of a growing list of imprints, including o-books.net and zero-books.net.

Circle Books aims to publish books in Christian spirituality that are fresh, accessible, and stimulating.

Our books are available in all good English language bookstores worldwide. If you can't find the book on the shelves, then ask your bookstore to order it for you, quoting the ISBN and title. Or, you can order online—all major online retail sites carry our titles.

To see our list of titles, please view www.Circle-Books.com, growing by 80 titles per year.

Authors can learn more about our proposal process by going to our website and clicking on Your Company > Submissions.

We define Christian spirituality as the relationship between the self and its sense of the transcendent or sacred, which issues in literary and artistic expression, community, social activism, and practices. A wide range of disciplines within the field of religious studies can be called upon, including history, narrative studies, philosophy, theology, sociology, and psychology. Interfaith in approach, Circle Books fosters creative dialogue with non-Christian traditions.

And tune into MySpiritRadio.com for our book review radio show, hosted by June-Elleni Laine, where you can listen to authors discussing their books.

MySpiritRadio